Pike:
an Introduction

The Pike Development Team

H. William Welliver and Martin Bähr, Editors

 The Chestnut Press ❧ Baltimore

Foreword

Once upon a time, there was a little language called SETL. Its basic idea was to provide a "high-level language" as an advance over low-level programming languages, such as C. The premise of SETL was that humans think in sets, in maps, in dynamic arrays - just like mathematicians have claimed for centuries. I think that SETL is beautiful, and I have always been fond of SETL programs. They look so clean, small, and crisp.

However, since a high-level language abstracts away many details of the underlying machine, SETL programs had problems being efficient. You can implement a set in many ways, and how you implement it may slow down or speed up your application enormously. Hence, SETL invested heavily in program optimizations, and some of the most advanced optimization technologies, such as R. Paige's program differentiation, were invented for it. However, this development took quite some time, and in the end, SETL was deemed to be inefficient. The masses went away to other "nice" languages, such as Ada, C++, and Java. You know how that story goes...

But you also know that now and then, Scandinavian students start little projects that revolutionize the world. Usually, it takes 10 or 15 years, but nevertheless, these heroes boldly challenge the big players (remember Linus?) In Pike's case, the student is Frederik Hübinette, who convinced a brave team at Roxen AB, to invest in the programming language he was writing. The idea was simple: base everything on sets, maps, dynamic arrays; make a fast compiler; generate fast code, use typing and other modern language constructs, and – attack the global players – Ada, C++ and Java. I think they got it right. I get the same kick again, as I did in the case of

Pike: an Introduction

SETL. But now, there is a good compiler, environment, and small but steadily growing community, just as it was with Linux some years ago.

SETL was a big project, running over several years. The project consumed a lot of money, and finally failed. Pike is a small open source project, and we believe it has a great future, due to the enthusiasm and foresight of its inventors and supporters. Bill Welliver is one of these supporters. He undertook the effort to publish a new Pike introduction, and we can only but congratulate him for his excellent work.

Enjoy Pike and your day.

Uwe Aßmann and Peter Fritzson
Programming Environments Lab (PELAB)
Institionen för Datavetenskap (IDA)
Linköpings Universitet
Linköping, Sweden

Preface

How to use this Book

This book has been written to provide an introduction to the Pike programming language. It is not intended to be a complete reference manual. It does not document all of the modules and libraries that come with the Pike distribution, except for what is necessary to explain the workings of the language itself. Additionally, many of the more "advanced" features of the language will not be discussed completely, if at all, though 90% of the language that you will use on a regular basis will be covered. We also assume that Pike has already been installed on your computer. Instructions for installing Pike may be found in Appendix B.

This introduction is mainly intended for people with at least some experience of programming, for example from writing some JavaScript on a web page, or CGI scripts on a web server in some language. We assume that you now have a need for, or perhaps just an interest in, using Pike. We recommend that you try to run the examples as you read them, since this will help your learning greatly.

Even total beginners at programming will be able to understand much of what is discussed in the chapters that follow. If you have never programmed before, it would be a good idea to read a general introduction to programming. There are some general skills and ways of thinking that are needed to write good programs, and a language introduction such as this one will not cover those in any depth.

We have tried to make this introduction platform-independent, meaning that it will not matter if you are using Pike under Linux, Solaris, Windows NT, or some other operating system. There are some situations where this is not possible, and in those cases we will point out the differences and how to deal with them.

Terminology and Typographic Conventions

In order to make the most of this book, it's important to understand the meaning of certain conventions employed in the text. This section will lay out some ground rules that will govern the formatting and use of technical terminology in later sections of the text.

When we discuss terms that may possibly have different meanings depending on the context, we will attempt to make the meaning clear in material leading up to its use, as well as in the presentation of the term itself. A good example of this technique occurs in situations where we are talking about a Pike construct. In these situations, we will use monospace characters to identify this, as opposed to a general term, which will appear in regular characters. For example, when you see the word object (note that we haven't used any special formatting), we are speaking of a generic bit of code, such as a variable or perhaps a generic data structure. However, when you see the term `object` (note the monospace formatting), you should understand that we are talking about the specific Pike datatype.

The following conventions for type faces are used:

Boldface is used for terms that have a special meaning.

Example:

>   A **variable** may be seen as a sort of box where you may store a
>   value. It can also be used to show values, such as **7.3**.

`Fixed size` type is used for something that is copied verbatim from the computer. It may be a Pike construct, part of a program, something printed by the computer, or something typed by the user.

Example:

> In Pike, the datatype integer is spelled `int`.

Italics are used for emphasis, and are also used as a placeholder for other things. When you see fixed type text with italics, it means that you should replace the italicized portions with a real program construct.

Example:

> In Pike, you can define a variable with "*datatype name;*", where you replace *name* with the name of the variable, and *datatype* with its type.

A bordered section of fixed-size text on a grey background represents an interactive session with the computer, where user input is marked in boldface italics. The rest of the session's text is program output:

```
Hello, professor.
I see you brought the keys to the ferarri.
> run project 21
Warming up particle accelerator...
```

Within fixed-width blocks of Pike code in Pike examples, changes are marked with a subtle shading, as in:

Listing 1: A code example

```
void example()
{
    write("This line was changed from the previous example.\n");
}
```

Book Website

Be sure to visit the companion website for this text, which can be found at http://book.gotpike.org. Once there, you'll find errata, related websites and supplemental code designed to enhance your experience with this book and Pike.

Acknowledgments

This text is an expanded and partially rewritten version of the Pike language tutorial originally prepared for Roxen Internet Software by Thomas Padron-McCarthy, based on an earlier tutorial by Fredrik Hübinette. The editors wish to acknowledge the assistance of James Tyson, Martin Nilsson and Johan Sundström, and many others, without whom this edition would not have been possible.

Table of Contents

Introduction

What you should learn from this chapter:

1. Be able to identify some of the major features of Pike

2. Understand some of similarities and differences that Pike has with other languages.

What is Pike?

Pike is an interpreted, object-oriented programming language. It looks a bit like C and C++, but it is much easier to learn and use. It can be used for small scripts as well as for large programs.

Some important characteristics of Pike include:

◆ High-level and powerful language constructs. Even very complex things are easy to do in Pike.

◆ Pike is an object-oriented language. Modern programming techniques can be used to divide a large program into small pieces, which are much easier to write than it would be to write the entire program at once.

◆ Pike is compiled at runtime. Compilation and execution are integrated into one step. Each file is only compiled when it is needed so you don't have to wait for a program to compile and link all files before you can run it.

Pike: an Introduction

- Memory is garbage-collected. You don't have to manually manage the memory used by a program. This makes programming much simpler, and minimizes the occurrence of memory leaks and other memory-related bugs.

- Pike is easy to extend. You can create plug-ins, written in Pike as well as in C or C++, and integrate them with the rest of Pike.

Pike can be used to write small and simple scripts, and also for very large programs. The Web application servers Roxen WebServer and Caudium are examples of large projects written in Pike. Pike's advanced data types and built-in support for sockets makes it ideal for use in Internet applications.

Pike is free software, distributed under the GNU General Public License (GPL), GNU Lesser General Public License (LGPL) and Mozilla Public License (MPL). Pike is available for many operating systems, among them Linux, Solaris, Mac OS X and Microsoft Windows.

Where did Pike come from?

Pike has been around for well over a decade, and has had an interesting life. In the late 1980s, multi-user adventure games were very popular. One of the people working on these games was Lars Pensjö at Chalmers University in Gothenburg, Sweden. For his game he needed a simple, memory-efficient language, and thus in the year 1988, LPC (Lars Pensjö C) was born. About a year later, Fredrik Hübinette started playing one of these games and found that the language was the most easy-to-use language he had ever encountered. He liked the language so much that he started improving it and before long had made his own LPC dialect called LPC4.

While LPC4 was still geared towards writing adventure games, it was quite useful for writing other things as well. However, a major problem with LPC4 was the copyright. Since it was based on Lars Pensjö's code, it came with a license that did not allow it to be used for commercial gain. So in 1994, with financial backing from Signum Support AB, Fredrik started writing μLPC. It was a new but similar LPC interpreter which was released under GNU GPL.

When μLPC became usable, a Swedish company called InformationsVävarna AB (which would later become Roxen Internet Software) started using it as a base language for a Web server they were developing. Up to that point, the software, called Spinner, was non-commercial and written in LPC4. Converting their code to μLPC allowed InformationsVävarna to produce Spinner as a commercial product. In 1996 Fredrik started working for InformationsVävarna developing μLPC for them. To get a more pronounceable and commercially viable name the language was eventually renamed from μLPC to Pike.

At InformationsVävarna, Pike was further developed by Fredrik together with several other employees, most notably Per Hedbor, Henrik Grubbström, Martin Stjernholm, Pontus Hagland and Marcus Comstedt. Not only did they improve, extend and optimize the language itself, but a lot of new modules were added. Other notable module additions came from Honza Petrous and Francesco Chemolli.

Near the end of 2001, partly because of Roxen's shifted focus from research and partly because of the high quality that Pike has attained, Roxen Internet Software began searching for a new maintainer for Pike. This call was answered by the programming environment laboratory at Linköping University, who took over the copyright and maintenance responsibility for Pike in 2002. Today, Pike is devel-

Pike: an Introduction

oped and maintained by an international team of developers who are dedicated to making Pike the best programming language of its kind.

What does Pike look like?

Now that you know a little bit about what Pike is and where it came from, you'll probably want to know what a Pike program actually looks like. Without further ado, here is a small Pike program:

Listing 1: A sample Pike Program

```
int main()
{
  write("Hi there! What's your name?\n");
  string name = Stdio.stdin->gets();
  write("Nice to meet you, " + name + "!\n");
  return 0;
}
```

You can type this program into a text editor, and save it in a file called myprogram.pike. Once you've done that, you can run it to get the following output:

```
$ pike myprogram.pike
Hello, what's your name?
James
Nice to meet you, James!
$
```

Programmers with some experience from programming languages such as C, C#, or Java will probably be immediately comfortable with the general syntax of this simple program and will not have much trouble understanding what this program does. Pike looks a lot like those languages, and for example uses the "curly brackets" "{" and "}" to organize program code into blocks. An excerpt from a Pike program usually does the same thing that a similar-looking program fragment in C, C# and Java would do. Exactly *how* it is done may be very different, though.

All those backslashes (that is, "\") and semicolons (;) may be a bit confusing at first. Getting comfortable with the syntax (that is, how a program looks on the surface) is often the most difficult part about learning a language, and Pike is no different in that regard. On the other hand, experience tells us that most people are productive and comfortable with this syntax once they have become used to it, which is why we keep this as it is.

Language Comparison

There are a lot of programming languages floating around out there, and sometimes you have to wonder, why? Each language has its own set of strengths and weaknesses. If you're familiar with some other language, it might be helpful to understand what makes Pike different.

C++ and C

Pike looks a lot like C++ on the surface. But because you don't have to worry about memory allocation, it's easier to use and harder to write a program that crashes mysteriously. Since it is interpreted, it may be slower for some applications. Pike is more flexible than C++, and allows for a somewhat less rigid programming style than what is necessary in C++. Another difference is that there are many different C and C++ compilers, while there is only one implementation of Pike.

Pike: an Introduction

C#

Pike is very similar to C#. In fact, one could easily think that some engineers at Microsoft and the other companies behind C# were Pike-users. The most noticeable difference between the two is probably the fact that Pike has better standard types than C# and doesn't require the use of libraries for type conversions etc. If you are using C#, you will find Pike very easy to use.

Java

Pike looks a bit like Java on the surface. Like Java, Pike is translated to an intermediate format, which is then executed by an interpreter. Java programs are usually distributed to the user in this intermediate format, but with Pike we use the source code. This is feasible since in Pike, compilation time, i. e. the time it takes to translate the program to the intermediate format, is negligible compared to the time the program takes to run.

Perl

Perl started out on Unix systems as a system administration tool and contains lots of syntax shortcuts that an expert Perl user can use to obtain results, primarily with string operations, with very little code. This rapid result approach has made Perl very popular for text processing operations. The syntax shortcuts, however, make it much harder to read. It is also typically harder to write larger applications or write fast programs and avoid bugs in Perl than it is in Pike.

Python

Programs written in Python look very different from Pike programs, but Python and Pike are similar when it comes to ideas and use. Python is more widely used and has more libraries available. Pike on the other hand is faster, has a more advanced type system, and supports more object-oriented programming constructs (most notably, it has better support for encapsulation and information hiding). Pike's C-like syntax makes it easier to get started with for programmers who know C++, C or Java.

In general, you'll find that Pike is well suited for most types of programming tasks, from small ad-hoc scripts to full blown applications. In cases where Pike isn't a viable option for a final product, its similarity to languages like Java and C make it an ideal candidate for use in preparing prototype and proof of concept applications.

Additional Resources

The Official Pike Language Website

> http://pike.ida.liu.se

The Pike Community Website

> http://gotpike.org

Website for this book, Pike: An Introduction

> http://book.gotpike.org

First Steps

What you should learn from this chapter:

1. Be able to enter and run a Pike program.

2. Use interactive Pike to communicate with the Pike interpreter.

Hello World

It is traditional to start a book or introduction about a programming language with a very simple example: a program that just writes the text "Hello world!" on the screen. Since we think that's a very reasonable tradition to keep, we'll start off with a version of "Hello World" written in Pike, shown in Listing 1.

Listing 1: Hello World

```
int main()
{
    write("Hello world!\n");
    return 0;
}
```

To run this program, you will write it in a text file, for example called "hello.pike", and then run it. If you are using a text-based interface, such as a Unix command shell or the Command Prompt Window in Windows NT, you can run the program by typing the command "pike hello.pike".

If you are using a graphical interface where the file is shown as an icon, such as the Windows Explorer or a graphical file manager in Unix, you may be able to run the

Pike: an Introduction

program by dragging its icon and dropping it on the Pike interpreter, or by double-clicking on the program icon.

When you run the program, it will print

```
Hello world!
```

on the screen.

Explaining the "hello world" program

Starting in the middle of this program, the line

```
write("Hello world!\n");
```

is the central part of the program. We are using the built-in function `write()`, which prints text to **standard output**. The standard output is usually the computer screen.

Between the parentheses after `write()` we have put the **arguments** that we send to the function. In this case, there is only one argument, the text `"Hello world!\n"`. The double quotes (") signify that it is a **string**, i.e. a sequence of characters. The combination "\n" is translated to a **newline character**, so the next thing that is printed on the screen after the greeting will come on a different line.

We cannot let a line like this stand by itself in a program. It must be contained in a larger construct called a **function** or **method**. We therefore enclose it in the function `main()`:

```
int main()
```

```
{
    write("Hello world!\n");
}
```

This (as yet unfinished) program means that there exists a function called `main()`, and that this function will print a greeting to the standard output as explained before. The `int` before `main()` means that (besides doing the printing) the function will also return a value, an integer, to whatever it is that uses it. But we have not specified which value it will return, so we add a line that does this, finally yielding the complete program:

```
int main()
{
    write("Hello world!\n");
    return 0;
}
```

When Pike runs (or "executes") a file like this one, it always starts by calling `main()`. When `main()` is finished, the program stops executing, and the returned value is used to indicate whether the program succeeded to do what it was supposed to do. Returning the value 0 from `main()` means success.

A semi-colon (`;`) signifies the end of a **statement**. This program contains two statements: the use of `write()`, and the returning of a value. In the good old days, statements would have been called "program lines", since you had to have a statement on each line, but nowadays most programming languages allow you to write in "free format", dividing your program into lines in any way that you feel makes it easy to read. There are still some constraints: you can't split words, and

Pike: an Introduction

you can't start a new line in the middle of a quoted string. Listing 2 is the same program as before, but rearranged.

Listing 2: Hello World, oddly arranged

```
    int
main (   )     {write   (
"Hello world!\n"); return


    0;      }
```

Those changes probably didn't make the program easier to read and understand, but there are many quite legitimate variations in how programmers choose to write. For example, listing 3 shows a common style.

Listing 3: Hello World, sensibly arranged

```
int main() {
  write("Hello world!\n");
  return 0;
}
```

I want my Greeting in a Window!

Pike has support for graphical user interfaces. If you have the GTK Pike module installed on your computer, you can use a slightly modified program to print "Hello world!" in its own window. This program is shown in listing 4.

Listing 4: A Graphical Hello World

```
int main()
{
  GTK.setup_gtk();
  GTK.Alert("Hello world!");
  return -1;
}
```

The statement "GTK.setup_gtk();" is a call to a function, similar to the call to write() in our first example. The function setup_gtk() is found in a module called GTK, so we must prefix it with "GTK." to let Pike know where to look for it.

The next statement, "GTK.Alert("Hello world!");", creates a small window, an "alert window", with the text "Hello world!" in it, and a button with the text "OK" in it.

When you click on the "OK" button, the window disappears.

The last statement in main() is "return -1;". In Pike, a negative return value from main() means that the program doesn't stop executing when main() is finished. This is necessary here, since otherwise the program would finish as soon as it had created the window, and the window would disappear at once.

However, now that the program doesn't stop executing when main() is finished, when does it stop? Never. We may close the window, but the program is still running. It doesn't actually do anything, but it is there.

One way that we can fix the problem is displayed in listing 5.

Pike: an Introduction

Listing 5: Graphical Hello World, refined

```
int main()
{
  object alert;
  GTK.setup_gtk();
  alert=GTK.Alert("Hello world!");
  alert->signal_connect("destroy", exit, 0);
  alert->show();
  return -1;
}
```

The Alert window created by GTK.Alert("Hello world!") is a thing, or an "object". It not only pops up on your computer screen, but you can also let your program do things with this object. For example, you can tell the window that when it is destroyed, it should order the entire program to exit. This is what the rest of of the statement does (even if we don't explain the exact details here):

```
alert->signal_connect("destroy", exit, 0);
```

Interactive Pike

You can use Pike interactively, which means that you type a line at a time, letting Pike execute it immediately. Just start Pike by giving the command pike, without any arguments. Then type a statement, for example:

```
# pike
```

```
Pike v7.6 release 6 running Hilfe v3.5 (Incremental Pike
Frontend)
> write("hello!\n");
```

Pike will then do what you told it to do, i. e. print "hello!" on a line:

```
# pike
Pike v7.6 release 6 running Hilfe v3.5 (Incremental Pike
Frontend)
> write("hello!\n");
hello!
```

Similar to main, the built-in function write() returns a value, which happens to be the number of characters it has written. Interactive Pike will also show you this return value:

```
# pike
Pike v7.6 release 6 running Hilfe v3.5 (Incremental Pike
Frontend)
> write("hello!\n");
hello!
(1) Result: 7
>
```

The return value from write() is the number of characters written, which in this case is seven characters; h, e, l, l, o, the exclamation mark, and the newline character. The one in parenthesis at the beginning of the line tells you that this is the first result, if you want to refer to it in subsequent expressions. Type help and press enter for more information about how to use interactive Pike.

Running Pike interactively like this can be very useful when testing things, for example when you are following this introduction. It can also be used as a very advanced calculator. *But beware!* Some things don't work the same way in interactive mode as they do when you run a Pike program from a file. If you've tried running something in interactive Pike, and don't get the results you expect, and have investigated the problem thoroughly, chances are you've run into one of thise differences.

Exercises

1. Enter and run one of the "Hello, World" programs.

    a. Which spaces can you remove and still have a working program?

    b. Where can you add more spaces and still have a working program?

2. Start Hilfe and use it to calculate the sum of the following numbers:

    1   42   13   7

3. Use the built in help in Hilfe to find out how to access the last result.

4. Download or enter some Pike Programs (available from any of the Internet resources listed in the first chapter) and run them.

Your Second Pike Program

When you complete this chapter, you should be able to:

1. Access functions and datatypes from modules.

2. Use conditional statements to control program flow.

3. Use functions to split programs into smaller parts.

Your first Pike program, which was examined in the previous chapter, was a program that printed "Hello world!" on the screen. Your second Pike program will be a World Wide Web browser, just like Mozilla Firefox or Internet Explorer.

Well, perhaps not *really* like Firefox or Internet Explorer. Both of those are very large programs, and our browser will be a very small program. We will just make it advanced enough to connect to a World Wide Web server, download a web page, and then display it on the screen.

We start by creating a file, for example called webbrowser.pike:

Listing 1: A Bare Bones Program

```
// The Very Simple World Wide Web Browser
int main()
{
  write("Welcome to the Very Simple WWW Browser!\n");
  return 0;
} // main
```

Pike: an Introduction

This is almost the same program as the "hello world" program. The only difference is that it prints something else, and that we have added some **comments**. Two "slash" characters (//) means that the rest of the line is a comment. Comments are ignored by Pike, and are intended for humans who read your program.

Variables

The web browser must be told which web page it should download and display. As you may know, the "addresses" to web pages are called URLs (Uniform Resource Locators), and they look like gotpike.org or http://gotpike.org (where the second form is technically correct, but the first usually works, too).

We have added some code that lets the user type a URL, stores that URL in a variable, and also prints it on the screen as confirmation:

Listing 2: Getting input

```
// The Very Simple World Wide Web Browser
int main()
{
  write("Welcome to the Very Simple WWW Browser!\n");
  string url;
  write("Type the address of the web page:\n");
  url = Stdio.stdin->gets();
  write("URL: " + url + "\n");
  return 0;
} // main
```

There are four new things here:

1. We create a **variable** with the name `url`. This process is called **defining** a variable. The variable has the type `string`, which means that we use it to store strings in. A string is a sequence of characters.

2. `Stdio.stdin->gets()` is used to let the user type some text on the keyboard. When the user hits the return key, the text is returned as a string. (`Stdio.stdin->gets()` calls the function `gets()` in the object `stdin` from the module `Stdio`, but you don't need to worry about that just yet.)

3. We take that string, and store it in the variable. This is called **assignment**, in other words, we **assign** a value to the variable.

4. In the last line with `write()`, we concatenate, or add, three strings together:

   `"URL: " + url + "\n"`

When we run the program, it may look something like this:

```
$ pike webbrowser.pike
Welcome to the Very Simple WWW Browser!
Type the address of the web page:
http://pike.ida.liu.se/
URL: http://pike.ida.liu.se/
```

An appropriate next step would be making your program run without the need for manually invoking it with the Pike parser. If you are using a Unix system, such as Linux or Solaris, you can make the web browser a free-standing program by adding:

```
#!/usr/local/bin/pike
```

Pike: an Introduction

(or "#!"followed by whatever Pike itself happens to be called on your system) as the very first line in the file, without any spaces in the part pointing out the path to your pike binary.

Assuming you want your script to run with whatever "pike" binary would be run if "pike" was entered at the prompt, that is, the first "pike" executable found in the user's path, a useful and portable alternative is this syntax:

```
#!/usr/bin/env pike
```

Either way, you must finish off the work by making the file executable:

```
$ chmod a+x webbrowser.pike
```

Now, you can run the web browser just by giving the command:

```
$ ./webbrowser.pike
```

or by clicking on its icon in a graphic file manager. (If you don't like the extension .pike, you can simply change the name of the file to webbrowser, without the extension.)

Under Windows NT, you can associate the file extension .pike with the Pike interpreter. Then you can start the web browser by clicking on the web browser's icon, or by giving the command webbrowser.pike in the Command Prompt Window. Usually the association is done automatically during installation of Pike, so normally this will work directly. Be aware that you may not be able to read any output or errors in such case, as the window will just disappear when the program exits.

Conditional statements

Before we let the program actually do anything with the URL we give to it, we will improve the program to let it take the URL as a **command-line argument**. That is, we want to start the program with the command

```
$ ./webbrowser.pike http://pike.ida.liu.se/
```

instead of letting the program ask for the URL. We add some code for this:

Listing 3: Slightly more sophisticated startup

```
#!/usr/local/bin/pike
// The Very Simple World Wide Web Browser
int main(int argc, array(string) argv)
{
  write("Welcome to the Very Simple WWW Browser!\n");
  string url;
  if(argc == 2)
    url = argv[1];
  else
  {
    write("Type the address of the web page:\n");
    url = Stdio.stdin->gets();
  }
  write("URL: " + url + "\n");
  return 0;
} // main
```

Pike: an Introduction

This program can handle a command-line argument, but if you don't give one, it will ask for an URL just as before.

There are some new things to explain here:

1. The line `#!/usr/local/bin/pike` only works on a Unix system, as described earlier. Pike running in Windows environments will ignore this line, so it may be left intact.

2. We have added `int argc` and `array(string) argv` as **parameters** to `main()`. These parameters are like normal variables, except that they will be assigned some values automatically when the program starts.

3. The variable `argc` has the type `int`, which means **integer**. It will contain the number of command-line arguments. The program name is counted as an argument, so if you give one argument to the program, `argc` will have the value **2**.

4. The variable `argv` will contain the arguments. Its type is `array(string)`, which means **array of strings**. Each command-line argument is put in a string, and together they form a list or array.

5. `argc == 2` is a comparison. We want to see if the value of `argc` is equal to **2**. `==` is an **operator** that checks if two things are the same. Some other comparison operators in Pike are `<` (less than), `>` (greater than or equal), and `!=` (not same).

6. `argv[1]` retrieves an element from position number 1 inside an array. The positions are numbered from 0, so position 1 is actually the second element in the

array. This is the URL given as argument to the program. `argv[0]` contains the name of the program, the string `"webbrowser.pike"`.

7. The `if` statement lets Pike choose between different actions. It follows the template or pattern:

```
if( condition )
  something
else
  something-else
```

If the *condition* (in our case, that `argc == 2`) is **true**, Pike will do *something*. If the *condition* is **false**, it will do *something-else*. In our program, there are two **statements** for *something-else*, so we must enclose them in curly brackets, { and } to form a **block**. This will be explained in detail in the chapter about statements.

Functions

We will soon add the web functionality, and actually download the web page. But the function `main()` is getting a bit long now, so perhaps it is time to divide our program into several functions. Instead of putting the web stuff in `main()`, we write a function called `handle_url()`, which will do all the handling of a URL.

```
void handle_url(string this_url)
{
  write("URL: " + this_url + "\n");
} // handle_url
```

So far, it only writes the URL on the screen, just like we did in `main`.

Pike: an Introduction

Some interesting things to note:

`main()` returns an integer, to indicate if the program succeeded or not. We don't care if `handle_url()` fails, so we set the **return type** of this function to `void`, which means "nothing".

`main()` had two parameters. `handle_url()` only has one: `this_url`. `this_url` may contain a string.

For this function to be executed by Pike, we must **call** it from `main()`. We replace the statement that printed the URL with:

```
handle_url(url);
```

This sends the value in the variable `url`, which is a local variable in `main()`, to `handle_url()`, where it will be put in the variable `this_url`. The thing that is sent, `url`, is usually called an **argument**, and the variable that receives it, `this_url`, is usually called a **parameter**.

Our program does have a problem. What happens if the user doesn't give an argument, and then just hits the return key when the program asks for a URL? `Stdio.stdin->gets()` will return an empty string, just as it should, but that is not a valid web address, and our browser will surely fail when it tries to retrieve the page. If we want the program to keep asking until it gets a non-empty answer, we can put the two ask-and-read statements inside a **loop**:

```
do
{
    write("Type the address of the web page:\n");
```

```
    url = Stdio.stdin->gets();
} while(sizeof(url) == 0);
```

This is a **do-while loop**, and such a loop follows the pattern

```
do something
    while( condition );
```

The do-while loop will do *something* at least once, and then keep doing it as long as the *condition* is true. First it does *something*, then it checks the *condition*, and then it either leaves the loop and continues after it, or goes back to the start of the loop and does *something* again. In our case, the *condition* is that `sizeof(url) == 0`, i. e. that the string `url` is empty.

Another problem with our program is that it only checks if `argc` is 2. If you give more arguments, the program will ignore them. We change the `if` test a bit, so that it prints an error message and then terminates the program if we give too many arguments. The complete program now looks like this:

Listing 4: The completed shell for our Web Browser

```
#! /usr/local/bin/pike
// The Very Simple World Wide Web Browser
void handle_url(string this_url)
{
    write("URL: " + this_url + "\n");
} // handle_url


int main(int argc, array(string) argv)
{
```

Pike: an Introduction

```
write("Welcome to the Very Simple WWW Browser!\n");
string url;
if(argc == 1)
{
  do
  {
    write("Type the address of the web page:\n");
    url = Stdio.stdin->gets();
  } while(sizeof(url) == 0);
}
else if(argc == 2)
{
  url = argv[1];
}
else
{
  write("Too many arguments. Goodbye. Sorry.\n");
  return 1;
}
handle_url(url);
return 0;
} // main
```

Note how we have chained two `if` statements together using `else if`.

Neither the curly brackets around `url = argv[1];` nor those around the `do` loop are necessary, since they only enclose a single statement each, but some programmers feel that it is better to be on the safe side having them there either way, in case they would add yet another statement later on and forget about adding the braces. Others feel that if you have curly brackets around one of the possible cases in an `if` statement, you should have curly braces around all of them. Uniformity makes it easier to grasp the structure of the whole thing at a glance.

Also note how the use of **indentation**, i. e. the varying amount of white space at the beginning of each line, makes it easy to follow the "block structure" of the program. For example, you can easily see that the **do-while** loop is inside the first case of the `if` statement.

Now it's time to start surfing the web! Perhaps you know that web pages are written in something called HTML (HyperText Markup Language), and that the "http" you see in web addresses like *http://pike.ida.liu.se/* means HyperText Transfer Protocol. The HyperText Transfer Protocol is a description of how web browsers communicate with web servers. Netscape and Internet Explorer use it, and so will we.

It is actually a fairly complicated operation to connect to a web server, to tell it to send you a web page, and then to receive that page as the server sends it. Fortunately for us, someone has already done the work for us. There is a **module** called `Protocols.HTTP`, which handles the communication with the web server. A module is a package of Pike code that may easily be used in other programms.

We rewrite the function `handle_url()` to actually try to fetch the web page, using the module `Protocols.HTTP`, as shown in Listing 5.

Pike: an Introduction

```
void handle_url(string this_url)
{
  write("Fetching URL '" + this_url + "'...");
  Protocols.HTTP.Query web_page;
  web_page = Protocols.HTTP.get_url(this_url);
  if(web_page == 0)
  {
    write(" Failed!\n");
    return;
  }
  write(" Done.\n");
} // handle_url
```

The interesting part here is the lines

```
  Protocols.HTTP.Query web_page;
  web_page = Protocols.HTTP.get_url(this_url);
```

First we define the variable web_page, with the data type Protocols.HTTP.-Query. Actually, the data type is called Query, and is defined in the module Protocols.HTTP, but we must write it as Protocols.HTTP.Query so that Pike knows where to find it.

A data item of the type Protocols.HTTP.Query contains the result of a web page retrieval: the text of the web page, but also some more information, such as the time when the page was created.

The actual work is done by the function `Protocols.HTTP.get_url()`, which is actually the function `get_url()` in the module `Protocols.HTTP`. It talks to the web server, fills a `Query` object with everything it finds, and returns it. If it cannot find the web page, it returns zero (**0**) instead.

Some other things that might need to be explained in this example:

1. We can use single quotes (`'`) inside a string. If we want to put a double quote (`"`) in a string, we may do so by prefixing the double quote with a backslash:

    ```
    "This string contains a \""
    ```

2. If the web page couldn't be found, we use the statement `return;` to stop executing the function `handle_url()`, and instead return to where it was called from. This is the same as the `return 0;` we have seen in main, except that handle_url doesn't return a value.

3. `return` just returns from the function we are in. If we want to terminate the program, we can use the built-in function `exit()` as `exit(0);` which has the same effect as returning **0** from main.

    When we run this version of the web browser, it may look something like this. The user's command is shown in *italics*:

    ```
    $ ./webbrowser.pike pike.ida.liu.se
    Welcome to the Very Simple WWW Browser!
    Fetching URL 'pike.ida.liu.se'... Done.
    ```

Pike: an Introduction

Now, if we try to retrieve a web page that doesn't exist, the web browser fails and prints an error message:

```
$ ./webbrowser.pike cod.ida.liu.se
Welcome to the Very Simple WWW Browser!
Fetching URL 'cod.ida.liu.se'... Failed!
```

Importing a Module

If we don't want to write the module name every time we use something from that module, an alternative is to **import** the module. Importing a module into your code brings the namespace of that module into your code. If we import Protocols.HTTP, we can use the data type Query, and the function get_url(), without prefixing them with Protocols.HTTP:

```
import Protocols.HTTP;


void handle_url(string this_url)
{
  write("Fetching URL '" + this_url + "'...");
  Query web_page;
  web_page = get_url(this_url);
  if(web_page == 0)
  {
    write(" Failed.\n");
    return;
  }
  else
```

```
    write(" Done.\n");
} // handle_url
```

The use of import is a popular technique in languages such as Java, though it's not widely employed in Pike. Although you *could* import lots and lots of modules for the ease of lazy typing, for the most part this is not a recommended practice, for obvious reasons of clarity and readability. There are also some non-obvious reasons to refrain from doing imports. If someone adds the function write() to the module Protocols.HTTP we would call that function instead of the one that writes text to the user. It also takes longer to start the program, since Pike must search through all imported modules to find the functions you use.

Initial Values for Variables

We can give a value to a variable when we define it, so instead of writing:

```
Query web_page;
web_page = get_url(this_url);
```

We change it to:

```
Query web_page = get_url(this_url);
```

A web browser that just prints "Done" instead of the web page isn't of much use, so now we should add some lines at the end of the function handle_url() to print the content of the web page:

```
void handle_url(string this_url)
{
    write("Fetching URL '" + this_url + "'...");
    Query web_page = get_url(this_url);
```

Pike: an Introduction

```
if(web_page == 0)
{
  write(" Failed.\n");
  return;
}
write(" Done.\n");
write("This is the content of '" + this_url + "':\n\n");
string page_content = web_page->data();
write(page_content + "\n");
} // handle_url
```

The interesting part here is the expression

```
web_page->data()
```

where we call the function `data()` in the data item `web_page`. This function returns the content of the web page, i. e. the HTML code, as a string. We then print that string.

Functions in data items?

"But", you say, "what is all this about a function in a data item? I thought functions were pieces of code that were parts of a program?"

Well, a function *is* a part of a program, just as we have seen. But just as our web browser contains functions, other programs can contain functions. And the "data type" `Protocols.HTTP.Query` is actually another program. The big difference is that it doesn't have a function called main(), so it can't be used by itself. It can only be used as a part of another program, as we have done here.

Somewhere on your computer there is a file, called something like

`/opt/pike/lib/modules/Protocols.pmod/HTTP.pmod/Query.pike`

on a unix system, or if you're using Windows, it might be something like:

`C:\Pike\lib\pike\modules\Protocols.pmod\HTTP.pmod\Query.pike`

Note that the actual location of the file will depend on where you chose to install Pike. This file contains the program Query with all its functions and variables, among them the function data().

A program like Query, which can be used in other programs in the way we have seen, is called a **class**. You can read more about how to use, and create, classes in the chapter about **object-oriented programming**.

Some Notes About WWW

When our simple web browser prints a web page, it just prints the raw HTML code. All the things between < and > characters are called *tags*, and they contain commands that indicate how the rest of the text should be formatted. To do that is well beyond the scope of this introduction.

Some web addresses don't refer to HTML pages, but to (among other things) sound clips or pictures. If you try to access such a web address with this browser, it will dump the sound or picture on the screen as if it had been text, and this will look even uglier than raw HTML code. Real web browsers check the type of the web page, and then take the appropriate action depending on that type.

If your web browser fails to retrieve a web page that you think exists, this may be because you haven't typed the address exactly as required. For example, some addresses must have a slash (/) at the end. More advanced web servers negotiate things like this with the web browser, and they usually manage to fix the address for you. You may not get a "failed" message when you try to retrieve a web page that doesn't exist. When the web server gets a request for a non-existent page, it generates a new web page with an error message, and your web browser receives and shows that page.

Listing 6: The Completed Web Browser

```
import Protocols.HTTP;
// The Very Simple World Wide Web Browser
void handle_url(string this_url)
{
  write("Fetching URL '" + this_url + "'...");
  Query web_page = get_url(this_url);
  if(web_page == 0)
  {
    write(" Failed.\n");
    return;
  }
  write(" Done.\n");
  write("This is the content of '" + this_url + "':\n\n");
```

```
    string page_content = web_page->data();
    write(page_content + "\n");
} // handle_url


    write("Welcome to the Very Simple WWW Browser!\n");
    string url;
    if(argc == 1)
    {
        do
        {
            write("Type the address of the web page:\n");
            url = Stdio.stdin->gets();
        } while(sizeof(url) == 0);
    }
    else if(argc == 2)
    {
        url = argv[1];
    }
    else
    {
        write("Too many arguments. Goodbye. Sorry.\n");
        return 1;
    }
    handle_url(url);
    return 0;
}
```

Pike: an Introduction

Exercises

1. Enter and run the complete program as presented in Listing 6.

2. What happens if you try to get the web browser to fetch a non-existent web page?

3. Modify the program to display the size of the web page retrieved as part of its output.

Basics of Pike Programs

At the end of this chapter, you should be able to:

1. Identify the various components of a Pike program and identify syntax errors in a Pike program.

2. Explain the difference between various zeros and why any type can have the value of an integer zero.

3. Explain what a reference type is and how it behaves differently than a basic type.

Pike works with **data items**, or **values**, such as the integers **17** and **-4717**, or the string of characters "**Hello world!**". Each data item has, or "is", a certain type: **17** and **-4717** both have the type **integer**, and "Hello world!" has the type **string**. If we want to refer to the data type **integer** in a Pike program, we write `int`. For the type **string**, we write `string`.

Each variable, function, and function parameter also has a type. The type determines which data items you can put in the variable, return from the function, or use as an argument to a function. An integer variable, created with

```
int i;
```

may only contain integer values. If we try to put something else, such as a string, in this variable, Pike will try to discover the discrepancy and complain about it. This is called type checking.

Pike: an Introduction

Both `string` and `int` are **built-in types** in Pike. You can also create your own data types, or **classes**. We have already seen some examples of this, for example the class `Query`, which is part of the module `Protocols.HTTP`, and which is used to contain the data we get when we retrieve a page from the World Wide Web.

We will examine each individual data type in some detail in a later chapter, but this chapter will give an introduction to data types in general.

Different Kinds of Types

The data types in Pike can be divided into three categories: the **basic types** (`int`, `float`, and `string`), the **container type**s (`array`, `mapping`, `multiset`), and then the types `object`, `program`, `function` and `mixed`. We will start by looking at the basic types.

We have already seen integers (`int`) and strings (`string`) being used in several examples, but the third basic type, `float`, is new. A `float`, also called a **real number** or a **floating-point number**, is different from an integer in that it can have a fraction part:

```
6.783    // This is a floating-point number

17       // This is an integer

17.0     // This is a floating-point number
```

Note that Pike differentiates between integer and floating-point numbers that happen to have a fraction part of 0. If you write `17` in a Pike program you get an integer, and if you write `17.0` you get a floating-point number. Inside the computer they look completely different, and when you compare them they are not equal.

You can define variables like this:

```
int number_of_monkeys;   // An integer variable

float z = -16.2;         // A floating-point variable

string file_name;        // A string variable

mixed x;                 // A variable for anything
```

The data type mixed means "value of any type."

Some of the data types are **containers**. A data item of one of these container types can contain other data items.

The simplest container type is the **array**. If a variable is a box where you can put a data item, then an array is a whole sequence of such boxes. The boxes are numbered, starting with 0, so in an array with 10 places the first one has number 0, and the tenth and last one has number 9. The position numbers are called **indices**.

You can give an array in your Pike program by listing its elements inside parenthesis-curly-bracket quotes:

```
({ "geegle", "boogle", "fnordle blordle" })

({ 12, 17, -3, 8 })

({  })

({ 12, 17, 17, "foo", ({ "gleep", "gleep" }) })
```

As you can see, an array can be empty (containing no elements), and it can also contain other container types. An array can contain elements of different types, but it is more common to use arrays that only contain one type of element.

Pike: an Introduction

You can define array variables like this:

```
array a;                // Array of anything
array(string) b;        // Array of strings
array(array(string)) c; // Array of arrays of strings
array(mixed) d;         // Array of anything
```

Then you can assign values to these variables:

```
a = ({ 17, "hello", 3.6 });

b = ({ "foo", "bar", "fum" });

c = ({ ({ "John", "Sherlock" }), ({ "Holmes" }) });

d = c;

d = allocate(9); // assigns an array of 9 elements initialized
to 0
```

You can access the elements in an array, either to just get the value or to replace it. This is usually called **indexing** the array. Indexing is done by writing the position number, or index, within square brackets after the array:

```
write(a[0]);            // Writes 17

b[1] = "bloo";          // Replaces "bar" with "bloo"

c[1][0] = b[2];         // Replaces "Holmes" with "foo"
```

A common programming mistake involves trying to access a non-existent element of a datatype that is indexed. These are called "indexing errors." An example of code that will cause such an error might be:

```
array fruits = ({ "apples", "oranges", "pears"});

fruits[0] = "grapes";   // Replaces "apples" with "grapes".

fruits[3] = "banannas"; // Element 3 doesn't exist.
```

The third line of this example will cause an indexing error because we try to put something in element 3 of an array that only has elements 0 through 2 (remember that arrays are numbered starting with zero). You can't access elements of an array that haven't been allocated to that array.

There are many useful operations that can be done with arrays. For example, you can add two arrays together:

```
({ 7, 1 }) + ({ 3, 1, 6 })
```

The result of that expression is a new array, with the elements from the two arrays concatenated:

```
({ 7, 1, 3, 1, 6 })
```

We can also subtract elements and take subsets of arrays (and other data types, too) by using basic operators, which will be described more fully in a later chapter.

In addition to arrays, there are two other container types in Pike, mapping and multiset. A set is something where a value is either a member or not, and a multiset is a set which can contain several copies of the same value. Mappings let you translate from one value (such as "beer") to another value ("cerveza"). Academics might know this datatype by the name "associative array", Perl programmers call them "hashes", and in Python the term dictionary is used. Mappings and multisets are explained in a later chapter.

Object, Program and Function

These three data types will be described in more detail later, but here is a short explanation of what they are good for.

Pike: an Introduction

An `object` is an entity that contains functions and the values of a bunch of member variables as defined by a program (or **class**, as a C++ or Java or Smalltalk programmer would say). An object is an instance of the **program**.

Just as we want to store objects in variables, and send them back and forth to functions, we sometimes want to do the same with a **program itself**. For example, we may need a function that creates an instance (that is, an object) of any program, and we must therefore be able to send the program as an argument to the function. This is what the data type `program` is used for.

Having a special datatype for Pike programs is very useful, and adds a lot of flexibility to Pike.

Something else that may surprise you is that there is a data type for **functions**. Sometimes you want to refer to "any function". Take for example the built-in function `map()`, which is used to apply an operation to all the elements in an array. You call `map()` with (at least) two arguments: the array to go through, and the function to call for each element:

```
void write_one(int x)
{
  write("Number: " + x + "\n");
}


int main()
{
  array(int) all_of_them = ({ 1, 5, -1, 17, 17 });
```

```
    map(all_of_them, write_one);

    return 0;

}
```

The first argument to `map()` is an array, and the second argument is of the type `function`. Running this code snippet would output:

```
Number: 1
Number: 5
Number: -1
Number: 17
Number: 17
```

Zero is special

The value zero (**0**) is a special case. It is not just an integer value, but can also be used to mean "no value" for all other types, except integers. If you create a variable and don't put a value in it, accessing it will give you the value **0**.

It's important to note that the integer value `0` and the real value `0.0` are not equal to one another in Pike. It is also worth noting that integers are automatically converted to strings when they are concatenated with strings. Uninitialized strings, as with all other uninitialized variables, return the integer `0`. If you don't take this into account, and write code that successively to a string, you might get unexpected results:

```
string accumulate_answer()

{

   string result;

   // Probably some code here
```

```
    result += "Hi!\n";

    // More code goes here

    return result;

}
```

you will get a string `"0Hi!\n"`, since Pike will try to make the best of the situation, adding your string to the integer 0. Had you instead initialized the variable to an empty string (`""`), as in `string result = "";`, you'd get a better result.

How to specify data types

In general, you just use the name of the data type:

```
int number_of_wolves;

Protocols.HTTP.Query this_web_page;

float simple_plus(float x, float y) { return x + y; }
```

You can also use the data type mixed, meaning any type of value:

```
mixed x;

array(mixed) build_array(mixed x) { return ({ x }); }
```

The variable x can contain any type of value. The function `build_array()` takes an argument of any type, and returns it inside an array.

For container types you may specify the types used inside:

```
mapping(string:Protocols.HTTP.Query) cache;
```

For integers you may specify a value range:

```
int(1..12) months;
```

Pike also lets you use "or" notation for datatypes, saying that a value is one of several possible datatypes:

```
int|string w;

array(int|string|float) make_array(int|string|float x)
{
  return ({ x });
}
```

The variable `w` can contain either an integer or a string. The function `make_array()` takes an integer, a string or a floating-point number as argument, and returns it inside an array.

If you know that a variable will contain strings or integers, it is usually better to use `string|int` than `mixed`. It is slightly longer to write, but it allows Pike to do type checking when the program is compiled and executed, thus helping you to ensure that your program works as it should.

Basic versus Reference Data Types

We have said before that a variable is a sort of box that can be used to store a value. But there is a difference between what we call "basic" values, such as integers, and more complex values, such as arrays. The basic values are stored in the variables, just as as we can expect, but the complex ones are not. They are stored somewhere else, and the variable only contains a reference to the actual data.

Usually, you don't need to think about this difference, but there are cases when it is important.

Pike: an Introduction

Here is an example to show exactly what the difference means. We start by defining an integer variable called i1:

```
int i1;
```

This variable can now be used to store integer values. We put the value **5** into i1:

```
i1 = 5;
```

If we could look inside the computer, this is what we would see:

Figure 1: A non-reference variable

```
int i1;          5
```

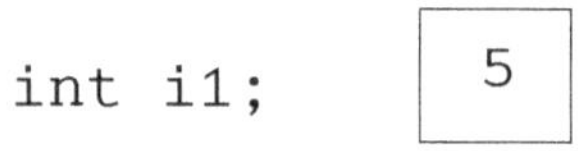

i1 is a box, which contains the value **5**. We now define another integer variable, called i2, and copy the value in i1 to i2:

```
int i2;
i2 = i1;
```

This is how it looks now:

Figure 2: Two non-reference variables, before the change

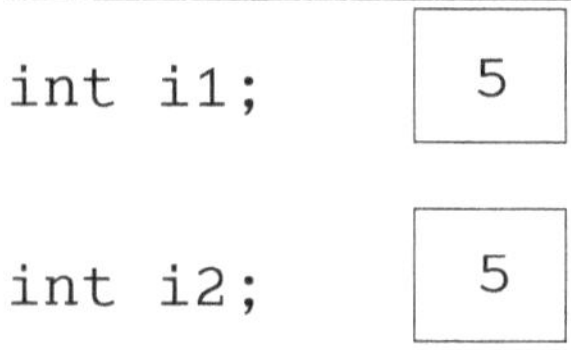

```
int i1;          5

int i2;          5
```

As we might have expected, there is a **5** in i1, and another **5** in i2. What happens if we change the value of i1?

```
i1 = 17;
```

Well, again as expected, the value in the variable i1 changes. The value in i2 of course doesn't:

Figure 3: Two non-reference variables, after the change

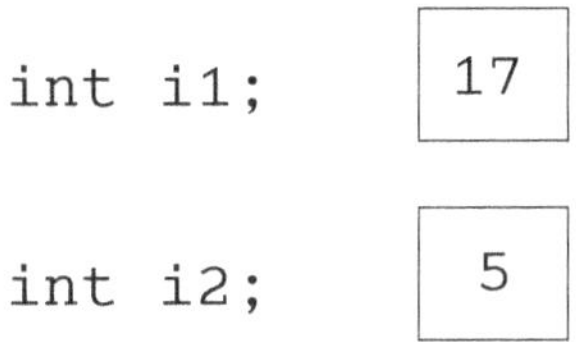

```
int i1;      17

int i2;      5
```

But with complex types, such as arrays, things are a bit different. To illustrate this, we define an array variable, a1:

```
array(int) a1;
```

This variable is of the type array(int), so we can use it to store an array of integers. So let's do just that. We create an array, and put that array into a1:

```
a1 = ({ 19, 3, 5 });
```

Inside the computer, it now looks like this:

Figure 4: A reference variable

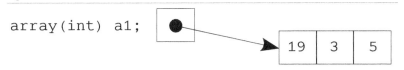

```
array(int) a1;
```

19 | 3 | 5

a1 doesn't actually contain the array, it just contains a "pointer" or "reference" to the array.

What happens if we try to do the same thing as we did with the integers above, that is, copy the value to a new variable, and then change the value in that new variable?

Pike: an Introduction

To show what happens, we define a new array variable, a2, and try to copy the array a1 to this new variable:

```
array(int) a2;

a2 = a1;
```

This is where things are different. Remember that the variable a1 doesn't contain the real array, but just a reference to it, and that an expression of the type

```
a2 = a1;
```

means "take whatever there is in a1, make a copy of it, and put that copy it in a2." Because of this, what gets stored in a2 is a copy of the *reference*, not of the array:

Figure 5: Two reference variables, before the change

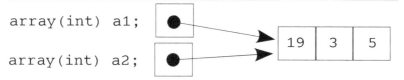

As a result both a1 and a2 now point to the same array. If we now try to change a2, for example by changing the last element in a2 from **5** to **17**:

```
a2[2] = 17;
```

what will change is the array pointed to by the reference in a2:

Figure 6: Two reference variables, after the change

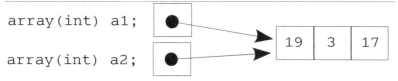

If we don't think about the fact that a1 and a2 just contain references, pointing to the same array, it would seem as if our change to the variable a2 had, in some mysterious way, also changed the contents of the variable a1!

If we want a real copy, and not just a reference to the same array, we must create that copy explicitly. We may use the function `copy_value` for this:

```
a2 = copy_value(a1);
```

This will create a copy of the array, and store a reference to that copy in a2:

Figure 7: Two reference variables, pointing to different things

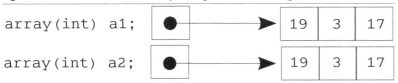

Note that `copy_value` creates a *recursive* copy, which means that if the array contains other arrays, it will create copies of those arrays too, and so on. A trick for creating a non-recursive copy of an array is to add an empty array:

```
a2 = a1 + ({ });
```

The result of the expression `a1 + ({ })` is a new array that is a copy of a1.

The following data types in Pike are **basic types**, and are stored in the variables themselves:

* int

* float

Pike: an Introduction

- `string`

The following data types in Pike are **reference types**, and what is stored in the variables are just references to the data objects:

- `array`

- `mapping`

- `multiset`

- `program`

- `object`

- `function`

Note that the same difference applies to function calls. When you send data to a function as arguments, and when you return data as the value of the function, what is actually sent is either the values themselves (for the basic types), or references (for the reference types).

Exercises

1. Prepare a program that creates a string by concatenating two other strings that are assigned to variables.

2. Prepare a program that generates an indexing error by accessing a non-existent element in an array.

3. Modify the program from exercise 2 so that the array is resized in order to avoid the indexing error.

4. Prepare and run a program that performs the following tasks:

   a) Creates an array and assigns it to two different variables.

   b) Shows that changing one array affects both variables.

   c) Copies the array and demonstrates that changing the copied array has no effect on the original array.

Functions

After you complete this chapter, you should be able to:

1. Describe how to write a function definition.

2. Explain what a side effect is and why it is important.

Most programming languages allow you to divide your program into smaller parts. These can be called "sub-routines", "procedures", "functions" or "methods". In Pike, we use the term "function" though you may also see "method" used interchangably. Other parts of the program may **call** the function, i. e. cause it to be executed.

How to create a function

To create a function, you must define it, with a function definition. A function definition follows this template:

```
access-modifiers type function-name( parameter-list )

{

  function-body

}
```

Pike: an Introduction

Here is a description of the various parts in the definition template:

- The *access-modifiers* are optional. If they are present, they control from where this function can be called. An example of an access-modifier is `private`, which makes it impossible for other programs to call this function.

- The *type* is a **data type**, which specifies the type of the value that the function returns. It is sometimes called the "return type of the function", or the "type of the function". If the type is `void`, the function is not supposed to return a value.

- The *function-name* is the name of the function. This is an identifier, for example `plus`, `destroy_all_enemy_ships` or `mUndoLatestChange`. A function should have a name that correctly describes what the function does: a function that prints a list of customers should probably be called something like `print_customers`.

- The *parameter-list* is a comma-separated list of the parameters of the function. A **parameter** acts like a variable, which is local in the function, and which gets the corresponding argument value from the function call as its initial value. Some examples of parameters are "`int number_of_cars`" and "`string name`". A function may have up to 256 parameters. If the function doesn't expect to receive any argument values, the *parameter-list* may be empty.

- The *function-body* is a **block**, and may contain statements and local definitions.

Sometimes we talk of the **head** and the **body** of a function. The body is of course the *function-body* in the template above, while the head consists of everything in the function definition except the body. We can say that the function head is a description of the function: its name, which arguments it expects, and what type of value it will return. A part of the program that wants to **call** a function, needs to know about the head of that function, but not about the body.

The **function body**, on the other hand, contains the statements that will be executed when the function is called. The body is therefore a description of what, and how, the function performs whatever it is that it does.

Here is a simple example of a function definition:

```
float average(float x1, float x2)
{
    return (x1 + x2) / 2;
}
```

The function `average()` returns the average of its two arguments. Both the return value and the two parameters are floating-point values. Here are some valid statements that contain calls to `average()`:

```
float x = average(19.0 + 11.0, 10.0);
average(27.13, x + 27.15);
float y = average(1.0, 2.0) + average(6.0, 7.1);
float z = average(1.0, average(2.0, 3.0));
```

When a function has completed executing the contents of its body it **returns**. The program will then continue executing immediately after the place of the function call. If the function has produced a value, that value is returned and may be used later.

Pike: an Introduction

The `return` statement is used to send a value from a function back to the point from where it was called:

```
return expression;
```

The `return` statement will also cause Pike to leave the function, and continue execution immediately after the point where the call to the function was made. You can have several `return` statements in the same function. If the function is defined to return `void`, you may use `return` without a value to leave the function:

```
return;
```

If you reach the end of the body of a function, without having returned first, the function will return without a value. If your function was defined as returning a non-void type, you must return a value.

Calling a Function

Functions are called by specifying the function-name and a comma seperated list of arguments inside `()`:

```
average(30.0, 10.0)
```

If the function takes no arguments the `()` remain empty:

```
average()
```

Usually a function produces a value, which you may assign to a variable:

```
float result = average(30.0, 10.0);
```

Pike allows you to provide an expression anywhere it expects a value. An expression is a piece of code that, when evaluated, will produce a value itself. This means that you can provide whole expressions as arguments to a function. Pike will evaluate those expressions, then pass the resulting value to the function before calling the function. For example, in the call:

```
average(19.0 + 11.0, 10.0)
```

the expression $19.0 + 11.0$ is evaluated, giving the values **30.0** and **10.0**. Then the argument values are sent to the function. If we look at the function head,

```
float average(float x1, float x2)
```

we see that it has two formal parameters. The argument values will be put in the two parameter variables, x1 and x2, which work as local variables within the function, but with the argument values as their initial values.

Execution will then continue with the body of the function. In this case, the body is

```
{
    return (x1 + x2) / 2;
}
```

The value of $(x1 + x2) / 2$ will be calculated, giving **20.0**. This value is then returned to the point where the function was called, and is used as the value of the function-call expression.

Here's another example which includes expressions as parameters to a function:

```
average(1.0, average(2.0, 3.0))
```

Pike will first call average() with the two values **2.0** and **3.0**, and when average() has returned the value **2.5**, it will send the two values **1.0** and **2.5** to average(). This second call of average() will return **1.75**, and this is the value of the entire expression.

More advanced examples of functions

Here are two more examples of function definitions:

```
int getDex()
{
  int oldDex = Dex;
  Dex = 0;
  return oldDex;
}
private void show_user(int|string id, void|string full_name)
{
  write("Id: " + id + "\n");
  if(full_name)
    write("Full name: " + full_name + "\n");
}
```

The function getDex() returns the value of a non-local variable called Dex, but also changes the value of that variable to zero (**0**).

The function show_user() expects to receive either one or two arguments. The first argument can be either an integer or a string. The second argument is optional, but if it is present it must be a string.

Here are some valid statements that contain calls to the two functions above:

```
getDex();
show_user(19);
show_user("john");
show_user(19, "John Doe");
show_user("john", "John Doe");
```

Side-effects in Functions

When working with functions, you may want to be careful with **side-effects**. A side-effect is anything that the function causes to change or happen, except for the returned value. Sometimes the side-effects are the reason for the function, and sometimes they are a dangerous misfeature. In the three examples above, getDex() has the side-effect of setting the value of the non-local variable Dex to 0, and show_user() has the side-effect that it writes some text to the standard output. We can guess that show_user() has been created just to write that text, so this side-effect of show_user() is probably not a problem. On the other hand, if a programmer uses getDex() to get the value of the variable Dex, it could come as a surprise that this function also changes the value.

Exercises

1. Prepare a function which returns the larger of two integer arguments.

2. Prepare a function which takes two arguments: the first, an integer and the second, either an integer or a string. If both arguments are integers, return the sum, otherwise, return the second argument.

Object-Oriented Programming

After you complete this chapter, you should be able to:

1. Describe some ways in which object orientation can save time and promote code reuse.

2. Describe some situations in which multiple inheritance can simplify development, and some situations in which it can be a hindrance.

3. Identify the various keywords and language components Pike uses to implement object orientation.

After half a century or so of computer programming, we have learned that **modularization** is a cornerstone of software development. Modularization, in this context, means that we divide a big problem into several smaller problems. Then we write a number of programs or program parts, each of them solving one of those small problems.

It is usually easier to jump one foot ten times, than it is to jump ten feet in one jump. In the same way, it is usually easier to write ten small programs, and then integrate them to a complete system, than it is to write the entire system at once. (Ok, we may expect some objections against that analogy. But the idea is the same in both cases, and it works in practice: small programs are almost always easier to write than big ones.)

The small programs or program parts are usually called "modules". Here, the term "module" is used in this general sense, but you should make a mental note that in

Pike: an Introduction

Pike, the term Pike **module** usually refers to a very specific kind of module, the plug-in modules of Pike.

For modularization to work well, we need something that is called **information hiding** or **encapsulation**. This means that we hide the internal structure of each module, so the rest of the system doesn't need to worry about it. Think of it this way:

If we build a locomotive in modules, we want to build one module at a time, and then bolt them together. If the cogwheels and stuff inside those modules are sticking out, outside the modules, the cogwheels in one module will jam the cogwheels in another module. The result is that the modularization doesn't work: even if we have divided the locomotive into modules, we still have to think about the cogwheels in all the other modules when we design the cogwheels in this module.

It is the same way with programs. The modules have lots of stuff inside: variables, loops, data structures. All of that should be hidden inside the module. Some programmers believe they should be so well hidden that it is impossible to look at them. Others feel that it is enough that you don't *have* to look at them. Remember: the cogwheels shouldn't be sticking out.

Obviously, we can't hide *all* the information. The modules must interact in some way, for example by sending data to each other. The (few) things that are visible on the surface of a module, for others to see and use, are also called its **interface**.

So how do we modularize a program? Which parts should we divide it into? One way is to look at what it does. You divide the thing it does into small things, and you divide those small things into even smaller things.

Another way is to look at the *data* that the program works with: simple things like numbers and strings of characters (in other words, text), and more complex things that may reflect real-world objects: persons, aircraft, or courses at a university.

For each piece of data, there are usually some functions that work with that data. For example, an aircraft has a passenger and cargo list, but also a limit of how many passengers and how much cargo it can hold. Each time a new passenger is added, it (or perhaps more correctly, the flight crew,) must check to see if the limit has been reached. The combination of data (what we know about something) and functions (what we can do with the data), is called an **object**, and each *type* of thing, like "aircraft", is called a **class**. As you may have guessed, this is the basis of **object-oriented programming**.

A class is the blueprint for objects. It contains the functions and fields for each piece of data. When we create an object, some pieces of data are set at that point. In our fleet we may have different sizes of aircrafts which can hold a different amount of passengers. Once the object is created (the aircraft is built), the number of seats does not change. The passenger list however, is updated for each flight.

An object is an **instance** or a **clone** of a class: all airplanes in our fleet are instances, or clones, of the class "Aircraft".

But to use object-oriented programming to its fullest, we need two more mechanisms: **inheritance** and **polymorphism**. Thanks to those, you can easily add features to an existing class. You can re-use all the work that was put into writing that class, and just add your new features.

Pike: an Introduction

If you need a class that describes birds, and you already have a class called `Animal` that describes animals, you can create a new class that **inherits** from the `Animal` class. By inheriting, a bird has all the attributes of an animal, and can do everything an animal can do. Then you just add whatever is specific to birds, such as flying. (Except that penguins don't fly, and bats do. We ignore that for now.)

Polymorphism means that whatever we can do with an animal, we can also do with a bird. If we already have some program code that counts animals or sorts them, we can use the same program code to count or sort birds, without changing anything. So not only can we re-use the work that was put into the `Animal` class: we can also re-use the work that was put into much of the rest of the program.

Programs Within Programs: Object-Oriented Pike

As we have said before, a **class** is a description of a type of thing. You can **clone** the class to create **objects**.

A class contains some variables, which are sometimes called **member variables**. The variables are attributes or characteristics of the objects, and each object will have its own set of the member variables. For example, if the class `Animal` has the member variables `name` and `weight`, then each animal will have those two variables, so each animal can have a name and a weight.

A class also contains some functions. (for other languages the terms "member functions" or "methods" are also used.) The functions describe things that the objects can do.

For example, if the class Animal has the function eat(), then you can call that function in any animal, to make it eat. Well, of course it won't really eat, since it's just some data in the computer and not a real animal. But the function can change the member variables, for example by increasing the value of weight for that animal.

Assuming that we have the class Animal, we can define some variables that can be used to store animals. Remember that the class is also a **data type**. We can also create some animals to put in those variables. To create an animal, we use the syntax *ClassName()*, i. e. the name of the class followed by a pair of parentheses.

```
Animal some_animal;
some_animal = Animal();
Animal my_dog = Animal();
```

To access a member variable in an object, we use the syntax *object_expression->variable_name*, i. e. the object followed by the operator -> followed by the name of the variable.

```
my_dog->name = "Fido";
my_dog->weight = 10.0;
some_animal->name = "Glorbie";
write("My dog is called " + my_dog->name + ".\n");
write("Its weight is " + my_dog->weight + ".\n");
write("That animal is called " + some_animal->name + ".\n");
```

Most objects need some initial values for its member variables. For example, every animal needs a name and a weight. One way to handle this is to set those variables separately, as we have done above. A better way is to design the class in a way that

Pike: an Introduction

lets it set the variables immediately when an object is cloned from the class. You can then give the values when cloning:

```
animal piglet = Animal("Piglet", 6.3);
```

We can call a function in an object, with a similar "->" syntax:

```
my_dog->eat("quiche");   // Real dogs eat quiche.
write("Its weight is now " + my_dog->weight + ".\n");
```

To create a class, you write a **class definition**, with all the member variables and functions. For the class Animal, which we have used above, the class definition may look like this:

```
class Animal
{
  string name;
  float weight;
  static void create(string n, float w)
  {
    name = n;
    weight = w;
  }

  void eat(string food)
  {
    write(name + " eats some " + food +".\n");
    weight += 0.5;
  }
}
```

Some explanations about this:

- A member variable, such as `name`, exists once in each cloned object, not in the class itself.

- When a function, such as `eat()`, refers to a member variable, such as `weight`, it will use that variable in the same object that it was called for. For example, when we call `my_dog->eat("quiche")`, it is the `weight` in the object `my_dog` that is increased.

- The function `create()` is special. This function that handles the arguments that you give when you clone an object. It is declared static because it is not supposed to be used from outside the object. (C++ programmers would call this a "constructor.")

- You can also have a function called `destroy()`. This function is what C++ programmers would call the "destructor", i. e. a function that is run just before the object disappears. A destructor is sometimes needed for cleanup, but is used much less often in Pike than in C++, since Pike has automatic garbage collection which will clean up when the data is not in use anymore.

Classes as Record Types

Sometimes you just need to group a few values together. This is called a "record" in Pascal, and a "struct" in C. You can use Pike's **class** mechanism for this too. Just create a class with the data you are interested in:

```
class Customer
{
```

Pike: an Introduction

```
    int number;
    string name;
    array(string) phone_numbers;
}
```

Then use it:

```
array(Customer) all_customers = ({ });
customer c = Customer();
c->number = 18;
c->name = "Ellen Ripley";
c->phone_numbers = ({ "555-8767", "555-4001" });
all_customers += ({ c });
```

Programs are Classes and Vice-versa

It may surprise you to know that you have already seen several class definitions in this introduction. If you have written a program in Pike, you have also written a class. This is because in Pike, programs and classes are the same, and the terms **program** and **class** are used as synonyms.

A Pike program in a file is a class definition. The functions that you have defined in the file are the functions of the class, and the global variables (that is, the variables defined outside the functions) are the member variables. Basically, the contents of the file get wrapped inside a "class { }".

To create the equivalent of the class `Animal`, which we defined above, we would need a file with the following contents. The file name can be "Animal.pike", but any name will work.

```
string name;
float weight;

static void create(string n, float w)
{
  name = n;
  weight = w;
}

void eat(string food)
{
  write(name + " eats some " + food + ".\n");
  weight += 0.5;
}
```

To make this program accessible to Pike it must be in the module search path. If it is in the same directory as your other code you can just use:

```
.Animal piglet = .Animal("Piglet", 6.3);
```

If you don't like the dot you may put that program in a **constant** with a different name:

```
constant Animal = .Animal;
```

Pike: an Introduction

Now you can use `Animal` as the class name, just as before:

```
Animal piglet = Animal("Piglet", 6.3);
```

A class may **inherit** another class. This means that the inheriting class (also called **subclass** or **child class**) starts with all the functions and member variables of the inherited class (also called **superclass** or **parent class**). The subclass can then have its own, additional functions and member variables.

One situation when inheritance can be useful is when you want to create two or more classes that have a common part. Birds and fishes, for example, are different, with different characteristics, but they do have much in common. You can make use of this by creating a class, for example called `Animal`, with the common properties. Then you define the two subclasses `Bird` and `Fish`, which inherit from `Animal`.

At other times you already have a class that almost does what you want it to, but you would like to add something to it. For example, a class `Connection`, which models an Internet connection, may have everything you need except for a time limit on how long you can be connected, You could then create a new class, `RestrictedConnection`, which inherits from the old connection class, but with the time limit added.

In both of these situations, we have what is also called an **is-a relationship**: a bird **is an** animal, a `RestrictedConnection` **is a** `Connection`. We recommend that you use inheritance only to model is-a relationships.

You use the keyword `inherit` to let a class inherit from another class. For example, to create the subclasses `Bird` and `Fish`, which both `inherit` from animal, you would write:

```
class Bird
{
   inherit Animal;
   float max_altitude;

   void fly()
   {
     write(name + " flies.\n");
   }

   void eat(string food)
   {
     write(name + " flutters its wings.\n");
     ::eat(food);
   }
}

class Fish
{
   inherit Animal;
   float max_depth;

   void swim()
```

Pike: an Introduction

```
  {
    write(name + " swims.\n");
  }
}
```

A bird like Tweety can do anything an animal can do, and it has all the data that an animal has. But it can also fly (the function `fly()`), and it has a maximum altitude (the member variable `max_altitude`).

Note that the class `Bird` has its own function called `eat()`. There was one in Animal too, but the new one **overrides** the old one, and will be used in all `Bird` objects. If you have a function in the subclass with the same name as a function in the superclass, the module in the subclass **hides** or **overrides** the function in the in superclass.

If you still want to call the function in the superclass, you can prefix the name with two colons (`::`). That is what is done in the function `eat()` : after fluttering its wings at the sight of the food, the bird will do the actual eating, and that is done with a call to `eat()` in the superclass.

You can now use our two new classes:

```
Bird tweety = Bird("Tweety", 0.13);
tweety->eat("corn");
tweety->fly();
tweety->max_altitude = 180.0;
Fish b = Fish("Bubbles", 1.13);
b->eat("fish food");
```

```
b->swim();
Animal w = Fish("Willy", 4000.0);
w->eat("tourists");
w->swim();
```

One thing that needs explaining is the last line in the example above:

```
w->swim();
```

The variable w is of type Animal, and that class has no function called swim(). But that doesn't matter, since Pike always looks at the **object** that is stored in the variable. In this case, Pike looks at the contents of the variable w, finds that it is a Fish, and then calls the function swim() in that object. Looking at the actual object like this is called **dynamic binding**. (The opposite, to just look at the type of the variable and ignore what's actually in it, would be called **static binding**.)

As we said, we used inheritance to express **is-a relationships**. But there are other ways of using inheritance, for example to simply get access to some functionality. If you write a program that needs to work with a file on your hard disk, we could inherit the file-handling class Stdio.File, and then use all the functions in that class as if you had written them in your own program:

```
inherit Stdio.File;
// ...
read();
```

Pike: an Introduction

This works, but we recommend that you create an object of the type `Stdio.File` instead, and call the functions for that object

```
Stdio.File the_file;
// ...
the_file->read();
```

The opposite is also possible. You can create a class that looks like another class without inheriting it. So you could create a `Mammal` that looks like an `Animal`, but it does not inherit `Animal`.

```
class Mammal
{
  string name;
  float weight;
  float height;
  static void create(string n, float w, float h)
  {
    name = n;
    height = h;
    weight = w;
  }
  void eat(string food)
  {
    write(name + " feeds some " + food +".\n");
    weight += 1;
  }
}
```

This class may be used anywhere, where an `Animal` is expected. why? Because it provides the same interface as an `Animal`. It has the member variables `name` and `weight` as well as the function `eat()`. When Pike tests if two objects are compatible, it does not look at the name of the class or its superclasses, but it looks at the implementation. Here Pike does not enforce an **is-a relationship**, but only a **looks-like relationship**.

Multiple Inheritance

Sometimes we want to inherit from two or more classes. This works in Pike (and in C++, but not in Java). You just write several inherits.

Let's say we have a class `Friend`, that represents a friend:

```
class Friend
{
  void cuddle()
  {
    write("Cuddle, cuddle, cuddle!\n");
  }
}
```

A hamster, as we all know, is both an animal and a friend, and it can also dance:

```
class Hamster
{
  inherit Animal;
  inherit Friend;
```

Pike: an Introduction

```
  void dance()

  {

    write(name + " dances.\n");

  }

}
```

So, try it out:

```
Hamster h = Hamster("Blue Lightning", 0.12);

h->cuddle();        // Cuddle as a friend

h->eat("grain");    // Eat as an animal

h->dance();         // Dance as a hamster
```

Access Control

Do you remember the discussion earlier about information hiding? In the examples above, everyone could access all the functions and member variables in all objects. For example, it is very easy to lose weight:

```
h->weight -= 10.0;
```

Oh? The hamster only weighed 0.12, and now it weighs *minus* 9.88?

We would like to control the access to the member variable `weight`, so that code outside the class cannot touch it. For uses like this, there are a number of **access modifiers**, which are written before the data type in the definition of a function or member variable. For example, the weight of an animal is represented by the member variable `weight`, defined as:

```
float weight;
```

By changing that to

```
private float weight;
```

,we only allow functions in the same class to access that variable.

The following is a list of the access modifiers available in Pike. Note that some have names similar to those in other languages, but they do not necessarily behave similarly.

public

This is the default, and means that any function can access the member variable, or call the function. All public members make up the interface of a class. This is the default access modifier.

private

This means that the member variable or function is only available to functions in the same object It will not be accessible to subclasses or other objects of the same class.

static

This means that this member variable or function is only available to functions in the same object. (static in Pike is like the external use of static in C and does not at all mean the same thing as static in C++. Instead, it is similar to protected in C++.)

local

This means that even if this function is overridden by a function in a subclass, functions in this class will still use this function.

Pike: an Introduction

final

> This prevents subclasses from re-defining this function.

optional

> This makes a member variable or function not be a required part of the interface.

If a class has a constructor (that is, a function called `create`) it is a good idea to declare it `static`. It is not supposed to be called except during the construction of the object, and if it is not `static` it will be part of the public interface of the class which must be matched when defining compatible (sub-)classes.

Exercises

1. Design a class to represent motor vehicles and one that represents a boat.

2. Implement each of the classes above.

3. Design a class for an amphibious vehicle that has the qualities of both a motor vehicle and a boat. Hint: consider using multiple inheritance.

4. Implement the design for the amphibious vehicle above.

Statements

When you complete this chapter, you should be able to:

1. Name the 3 classes of statements present in Pike and the differences between them.

2. Identify a block statement and its beginning and end points.

3. Describe pitfalls associated with use of ? : and the empty statement.

A *statement* causes the computer to carry out some definite action. There are three different classes of statements in Pike: *expression statements*, *control statements* and *compound statements* or *blocks*. This chapter will discuss each of these statement types and show you when to use each one.

The Expression Statement

An **expression statement** is something we are all familiar with, as we have used it in every chapter so far. It follows this template:

```
expression ;
```

That is, you just take an expression and put a semi-colon (;) at the end. Typical expression statements are:

```
write("Hello world!\n");

i = 7;

++i;
```

Pike: an Introduction

All of these are expressions with a semi-colon appended. Since the expression statement doesn't do anything with the value of the expression, it is the so-called " side-effects" of the expressions that we are interested in. For example, the expression "i = 7" has the value **7**, but what is interesting is of course that it has the side-effect of setting the variable i to **7**.

Since you can take any expression and add a semi-colon, these strange-looking (and rather useless) statements are also allowed:

```
2 + 2;
3;
```

Control Statements

A program must often make choices, choosing between different instructions to execute. Additionally, it often needs to execute the same instructions several times. All this is done using various **control statements**.

Pike has three facilities for choosing between alternatives: the **if** statement, the **switch** statement, and the **?** : operator. There are also several statements for repeatedly performing the same operation, such as **while, do while, for** and **foreach**. These statements are called **loops** and will be discussed in the second part of this chapter. Finally, there are some miscellaneous statements that don't fall into either of these categories that are discussed following, such as **return** and **catch**.

The if statement

You have already learned about the `if` statement, which is used to perform an action when a test expression evaluates to **true**. To recap, the `if` statement is formed in the following way:

```
if( expression )
   statement1
else
   statement2
```

Here is an example utilizing `if`:

```
if(sizeof(argv)>1)
   url = argv[1];
else
{
   write("Type the address of the web page:\n");
   url = Stdio.stdin->gets();
}
```

You can also "chain" multiple if-else statements together, such as:

```
if (expression a)
   ...
else if (expression b)
...
else
   ...
```

Pike: an Introduction

The switch statement

If your program must choose between a number of different actions, depending on the value of a variable or expression, you may express this using a chain of `if` statements. This is a modified version of a part from our browser:

```
if(argc == 1)
  write("Not enough arguments. Sorry.\n");
else if(argc == 2)
  url = argv[1];
else if(argc == 3 || argc == 4)
  write("Too many arguments. Sorry.\n");
else
  write("Way too many arguments! What are you trying? "
       "download the whole web?\n");
```

But in such cases a `switch` statement may be a better alternative:

```
switch(argc)
  case 1:
    write("Not enough arguments. Sorry.\n");
    break;
  case 2:
    url = argv[1];
    break;
```

```
    case 3:
    case 4:
      write("Too many arguments. Sorry.\n");
      break;
    default:
      write("Way too many arguments! What are you trying? "
            "Download the whole web?\n");
  }
```

In a switch statement, Pike first calculates the value of the expression between the parentheses, in this case argc. It then compares this value with all the values given in the cases in the body (i. e., between the curly brackets) of the switch statement. If it finds a value that matches, it jumps to that place and continues to execute the program there. It will then execute all the following cases until it gets to a break statement. A break statement will cause the switch to skip the rest of the code in the switch body, and continue execution after the block.

It is not necessary to have a default case, but if one exists, Pike will use that one if it finds no matching case value.

You can use a range of values in a case:

```
    case 10..14:
```

This case will match if the value is between 10 and 14, inclusively: 10, 11, 12, 13 or 14.

While on the topic of switch statements, it's probably worth mentioning that a very common (and very frustrating) semantic error is to inadvertently exclude a break statement at the end of a `case` block. While there are probably situations where this is desirable, it can often result in confusing program behavior. A good approach to avoid this problem is to write the `break` statement immediately after you write the `case` statement, then go back and fill in your actions.

The ? : operator

The operator ? : is similar to the `if` statement, but returns a value. Expressions that use the operator ? : follow this template:

```
condition ? then-expression : else-expression
```

Condition, then-expression and *else-expression* are three expressions. Pike starts by calculating the value of *condition*. If that value is **true**, it then calculates *then-expression*, and doesn't do anything with *else-expression*. If the value of condition is **false**, it calculates *else-expression*, and doesn't do anything with *then-expression*. The value of the whole construct is the value of the expression that was calculated: either *then-expression* or *else-expression*.

Using this operator, you can rewrite

```
if(a > b)
  max_value = a;
else
  max_value = b;
```

as

```
max_value = (a > b) ? a : b;
```

We recommend that you don't use the ? : operator, unless you have to, as it can result in difficult to read code, and potential operator precedence errors. It can be necessary when writing function-like macros, but that is beyond the scope of this introduction.

Repetition and Looping

Pike has three different facilities for repetition: the while and do while statements, the for statement, and the foreach statement.

The while Statement

The while statement does something as long as a condition is **true**. It follows this template:

```
while( expression )
  statement
```

Pike calculates the value of *expression*. If the value is **false**, it leaves the loop. If the value is **true**, it executes *statement*, and then it goes back to the start and calculates the value of *expression* once again, to see if we should run another iteration of the loop.

Example:

```
while(temperature < 200)
  heat_some_more();
```

Pike: an Introduction

This will keep calling the function `heat_some_more()` until the value of temperature is at least **200**. If temperature was at least **200** from the start, `heat_some_more()` is never called.

As always, *statement* can be a block, so we can have several statements that are executed in each iteration of the loop. This example will print the first five elements (element number 0, 1, 2, 3, and 4) in the array `argv`, each on its own line:

```
int i = 0;
while (i < 5)
{
   write(argv[i] + "\n");
   i = i + 1;
}
```

The do while Statement

Sometimes we don't want to do the test in a loop until after the first iteration of the statement in the loop. In those case we can use the `do while` loop, which you already have seen before. The `do while` loop statement follows this template:

```
do
   statement
while( expression );
```

Pike starts by executing *statement*. Then it calculates the value of *expression*. If the value is **false**, it leaves the loop. If the value is **true**, it goes to the start of the loop, executes *statement* again, and then calculates the value of *expression* once again, to see if we should run another iteration of the loop.

If we want the user to answer "yes" or "no" to a question, and we want to keep asking until we get either "yes" or "no", we could write a loop like this:

```
string answer;
write("Have you fed the cat yet?\n");
do
{
  write("Answer yes or no: ");
  answer = Stdio.stdin->gets();
} while(answer != "yes" && answer != "no");
```

The for Statement

The for statement does something as long as a condition is true, just like the while statement, but the for statement also has a place to put an expression that is calculated before the loop is started, and another place for an expression that is run immediately after the statement in the loop. The for loop follows this template:

```
for(init-expression; condition-expression; change-expression)
  statement
```

This is (almost) equivalent to this while loop:

```
init-expression;
while( condition-expression )
{
  statement
change-expression;
}
```

Pike: an Introduction

The `while` loop in the example above, the one that writes the element in an array, can be re-written as a `for` loop, like this:

```
int i;
for (i = 0; i < 5; i = i + 1)
    write(argv[i] + "\n");
```

As an extra feature, the definition of the loop variable can be put inside the `for` loop:

```
for(int i = 0; i < 5; i = i + 1)
    write(argv[i] + "\n");
```

In that case, the variable `i` is local in the `for` loop, and disappears when we leave the loop.

The foreach Statement

The `foreach` statement is a very powerful construct. It takes advantage of a feature of the language known as **iterators**. Iterators make it possible to use `foreach` on datatypes other than arrays, such as mappings and objects. Specifically, you can use this statement with `string`, `array`, `mapping`, and `multiset` data-items as well as any `object` that provides an Iterator interface.

The syntax of `foreach` is:

```
foreach ( container ; index-variable ; loop-variable )
    statement
```

Each element of *container* is looped over, with the value of the element placed in *loop-variable* and the index of the element placed in *index-variable*. The type of *index-*

variable will vary depending on the type of *container*. If *container* is an `array` or `string`, then *index-variable* will be `int`, but for mappings, *index-variable* might be of type `string`. Take the following code for example:

```
mapping fruit_colors = (["grape": "purple",
                         "banana": "yellow"]);
foreach ( fruit_colors; string fruit; string color )
  write(fruit + "s are usually " + color + "\n");
```

If we enter this fragment into Hilfe, we will get the following output:

```
bananas are usually yellow
grapes are usually purple
Ok.
>
```

Note that when using `foreach` with objects, the actual behavior will depend on the *iterator* defined by the object. **index-variable** or **loop-variable** are optional. In cases where you are only interested in one of them, you may leave the other out, keeping the semicolon:

```
write("For tonights desert we have: ");
foreach(fruit_colors; string fruit; )
  write("%s, ", fruit);
```

or, if your list of fruits is an array:

```
array fruits = ({ "bananas", "apples", "grapes" });
write("For tonights desert we have: ");
foreach(fruits;; string fruit)
  write("%s, ", fruit);
```

Pike: an Introduction

Before Pike had support for iterators, `foreach` could only operate on arrays. This old `foreach` has a different syntax, using "," instead of ";":

```
foreach(fruits, string fruit)
  write("%s, ", fruit);
```

You will probably come across this version in existing code, but for consistency we recommend not to use it.

As you can probably imagine, you can use `foreach` in many places where you might have otherwise used a `for` loop. A sort of backward example of how the previous fragment might have been written using a `for` loop is included below:

```
mapping fruit_colors = (["grape": "purple",
                         "banana": "yellow"]);
array fi = indices(fruit_colors);
for(int i=0; i<sizeof(fi); i++)
{
    write(fi[i] + "s are usually " + fruit_colors[fi[i]] +
"\n");
}
```

This code produces the same effect as the previous example, yet is considerably less straightforward than using `foreach`. Code such as this was the source of many trivial bugs, now made obsolete thanks to `foreach`.

Leaving a loop: break and continue

Occasionally you want to leave a loop somewhere in the middle, and continue executing the program after the end of the loop. You can use the break statement for this, as in this example:

```
while(1)
{
  string command = Stdio.stdin->gets();
  if(command == "quit")
    break;
  do_command(command);
}
```

break can be used in loops and in switch statements. It will cause Pike to "break out" of the loop or switch statements, and execution will continue after the loop or switch statement. continue, on the other hand, can only be used in loops. A continue statement will cause Pike to skip the rest of the body of the loop, going directly to the next iteration. For example, this loop will never call do_command() with an empty string as argument:

```
while(1)
{
  string command = Stdio.stdin->gets();
  if(strlen(command) == 0)
    continue;
  do_command(command);
}
```

Pike: an Introduction

Some programmers feel that `continue` is unnecessary and makes the code hard to read. A loop that uses `continue` can always be re-written without `continue`. Our example would look like this:

```
while(1)
{
   string command = Stdio.stdin->gets();
   if(strlen(command) != 0)
      do_command(command);
}
```

In addition to `break` and `continue`, here are at least three more ways of leaving a loop in the middle:

*   You can use the `return` statement to leave the entire function.

*   You can use `throw()` to throw an exception.

*   You can call `exit()` to terminate the program.

The Empty Statement

Sometimes you may need a statement that does nothing. The **empty statement** can be used for this. It just consists of a single semi-colon. For example, you may want the body of a loop to do nothing:

```
// Keep checking if it is finished, until it is
while(! finished())
   ;
```

Note that the use of the empty statement can get you into trouble, as it's very easily overlooked. As a matter of good style, you should avoid the empty statement. If for some reason, you must use it, you should always make a clear comment to indicate its presence and function.

The Block, or Compound Statement

As we have seen above, you can enclose several statements in curly brackets, "{" and "}". The result is called a **block** or **compound statement,** and can be used as a single statement. Here is one example:

```
{
  write("Hello ");
  write("world!\n");
}
```

Do not put a semi-colon (;) after the final bracket (}).

You can define variables inside the block. Such a variable is local in that block, and is available only to the program code written inside the block:

```
{
  write("What is your name?\n");
  string name;
  name = Stdio.stdin->gets();
  write("Your name is " + name + ".\n");
}
write("Your name is " + name + ".\n"); // this won't work
```

A block may also be empty, just as you can have empty statements:

```
{ }
```

Other Statements: return and catch

The return statement is used to leave a function, and also to return a value from that function:

```
return;

return x + 3;
```

You can read more about the return statement in the chapter about functions.

The catch statement is used to try to execute some Pike code, letting the programmer control what happens if there is an error:

```
mixed result = catch
{
  i = klooble() + 2;
  fnooble();
  j = 1/i;
};


if(result == 0)
  write("Everything was ok.\n");
else
  write("Oops. There was an error.\n");
```

Note the slightly unusual form of the catch statement. This is because you can use catch like a function to surround an expression, or to surround a whole block of code. We use the semicolon at the end of the catch block, as we can assign the result of the catch to a variable for evaluation later. You can read more about the catch statement and its companion, throw(), in the chapter about error handling.

Exercises

1. Name the various types of statements, and give a brief description of what each is used for.

2. Write a program that loops through an array of fruits: Apples, Bananas and Oranges using the for statement. For each fruit, print the name and its position in the array.

3. Repeat exercise number 2, using foreach instead of for.

4. Write a program that asks a user for the name of a fruit they'd like to eat. Use the switch statement to write a customized response based on the type of fruit: Apples, Bananas and Oranges. In the event a user types a fruit not in the list, tell them to pick a different fruit.

5. Experiment with catch, by writing code that purposefully throws exceptions (such as dividing by zero). Use interactive Pike to examine the value returned by catch.

Data Types

After you complete this chapter, you should be able to:

1. Name the built-in types available in Pike and identify some of their properties.

2. Use functions that allow you to determine the type of a given variable.

3. Identify some common operations that you can apply to Pike types.

Like any typed language, Pike has a set of data types that can be applied to variables. Some of these data types may be familiar such as integers or floats, some of the others might be familiar from using various packages and add-ons to existing languages (such as the Hash class in Java), but in Pike they are first level datatypes. These are the basic types in Pike:

- integer (written `int` in Pike)

- floating-point number (`float`)

- string (`string`)

They are basic in the sense that data items of these data types can't contain other data items. When a data item of a basic type is stored in a variable, it is the data item itself that is stored, and not just a reference to it, as explained earlier.

Pike: an Introduction

The Data Type int

Integer values (whole numbers) can be written in several ways:

- In decimal (that is, base 10) format, i. e. the normal way to write numbers, such as 78.

- In octal (that is, base 8) format, with a leading 0, such as 0116 (which is equal to 78 in decimal notation).

- In hexadecimal (that is, base 16) format, with a leading 0x, such as 0x4e (which is also equal to 78 in decimal notation).

- In binary (ones and zeros) format, with a leading 0b, such as 0b1001110 (which again is equal to 78 in decimal notation).

- As a character literal within single quotes, which will give the Unicode character value for that character. For example, 'N' will give the character code for the character N, which is equal to 78.

You can use normal arithmetic operations, such as addition and multiplication, with integers, but you can also consider integers as sequences of bits and, apply bitwise operations on them. These and many other operations are explained in the chapter "Expressions and Operators".

Integers in Pike can be very large. For small integers (up to the value which a computer can store in an integer, which is usually 2147483647 or 9223372036854775807), Pike will use the computer's own, hardware-supported way of representing integers. For larger integers, Pike will use "**bignums**". These are slower, but can be arbitrarily large. Just like the smaller integers, bignums are represented exactly, without any rounding errors. Thanks to bignums, Pike does not have an integer overflow problem like some other languages, where adding 1 to 2147483647 would give you -2147483648 instead of 2147483648.

As a programmer, you will usually not need to worry about the difference between bignums and smaller integers. There may however be some operations, for example certain functions in certain modules, that cannot handle bignums but work with smaller integers.

Pike provides a function that can be used to determine if a value is an integer:

  intp(*something*)

The function `intp()` returns **1** if the value *something* is an integer, otherwise **0**. Example:

```
if(intp(u))
   write("The integer is " + u + ".\n");
else
   write("It is not an integer.\n");
```

The Data Type float

Real numbers, which are numbers that can have a fractional part, such as **18.34** and **-1000.03**, are represented in the computer as **floating-point numbers**. Floating-point numbers can be used to represent very large numbers, but with limited preci-

Pike: an Introduction

sion. The number of significant digits is the same, no matter the magnitude of the value.

You can write floating-point values in two ways, as usual with decimals, or in **exponential form** with an e:

```
3.1415926535
```

```
-123.0001
```

```
12.0
```

```
1.0e6 // 1.0 times 10 to the power of 6, i. e. one million
```

```
2.0e-6 // 2.0 times 10 to the power of -6, i. e. two one-
millionths
```

```
-1.0e-2 // Minus one hundredth
```

Some special operations that relate to floating-point numbers:

*   Check if a value is a floating-point number

    floatp(*something*)

The function floatp() returns 1 if the value *something* is a floating-point number, otherwise **0**.

*   Round downwards

    floor(*float-value*)

returns a float that is equal to the largest integer less than or equal to *float-value*. For example, floor(7.6) gives **7.0** (and *not* the integer **7**). If you do want the integer value, you can use an explicit type conversion: (int)7.6 gives you the integer **7**.

- Round upwards

```
ceil(float-value)
```

returns a float equal to the smallest integer that is greater than or equal to *float-value*. For example, ceil(7.3) gives *8.0* (and *not* the integer **8**).

- Round to the nearest integer

```
round(float-value)
```

if the value of the fraction is less than five, then it is rounded down; if more than five, it is rounded up. If it is equal to exactly five then it is rounded toward the nearest *even integer*. For example, round(7.5) gives *8.0* and round(6.5) gives *6.0*.

The Data Type string

Strings are sequences of characters, and are written within double quotes (") in Pike:

```
"scorch"
"Hello world!"
"Woe to you, oh Earth and Sea"
""
```

The last one is the **empty string**. Special characters, such as the double quote character, need to be preceded by a backslash character (\):

- \" to get a double quote (") in the string

Pike: an Introduction

- \\ to get a backslash character (\)

- \n to get a newline character

- \t to get a tab character

- \r to get a carriage return

- \0 to get a NUL character, i. e. the character with character code 0

Here are some examples of strings:

```
"One line\nAnother line\nA third line"
"Strings are written within \" characters."
```

You can also use **character codes** instead of the characters themselves. If you write \d followed by a decimal (that is, normal base 10) number, it will be replaced by the character with that character code. The same goes for \x followed by a hexadecimal (base 16) number, and a single \ followed by an octal (that is, base 8) number. The \0 is actually an example of this. These four strings are identical:

```
"Hello world"
"Hello \d119orld"
"Hello \x77orld"
"Hello \167orld"
```

Some operations that you can apply to strings:

- Check if it is a string

```
stringp(something)
```

The function `stringp()` returns **1** if the value *something* is a string, otherwise **0**.

- Concatenation

Strings can be concatenated with the + operator:

```
string s1 = "Hello";
string s2 = " ";
string s3 = "world!";
write(s1 + s2 + s3 + "\n");
```

- Concatenation of string literals

String literals, who are strings within double quotes that are written in a program, can be concatenated by just putting them after each other:

```
write("Hello" " " "world!" + "\n");
```

Pike has many powerful built-in operations for working with strings. Read more about those in the chapter "Working with Strings", later on.

Container Types

There are three container types in Pike:

- array or "vector" (`array`)

- mapping, "dictionary", "hash" or "associative array" (`mapping`)

Pike: an Introduction

- multiset or "bag" (multiset)

A data item of a container type can contain other data items. The container types are also **reference types**: When a data item of a container type is stored in a variable, it is not the data item itself that is stored, but a reference to it.

The Data Type array

As described earlier in this introduction, an array is a container that can contain a sequence of elements. The elements are numbered from 0 and on.

```
array(string) b;      // Array of strings
b = ({ "foo", "bar", "fum" });
b[1] = "bloo";        // Replaces "bar" with "bloo"
```

As you can see, array literals are written as comma-separated lists inside parenthesis-curly-bracket quotes. The data type of an array that may contain elements of the data type *datatype* is array(datatype). The data type array(mixed) is therefore an array that may contain any type of values. It may also simply be written as array.

As with all Pike datatypes, an array variable that hasn't been given a value contains **0**, and not an empty array. If you want an empty array, you have to assign it explicitly:

```
array(string) a1;      // a1 contains 0
a1 = ({ });            // Now a1 contains an empty array
array(int) a2 = ({ }); // a2 contains an empty array
```

As described earlier, you can access the elements in an array, either to just get the value or to replace it. This is usually called **indexing** the array. Indexing is done by writing the position number, or **index**, within square brackets after the array:

```
write(a[0]);
b[1] = "bloo";
c[1] = b[2];
```

Note that the first position in an array is numbered 0 and not 1, and the second one is numbered 1, and so on.

A special feature is that you can use negative indices: `array[-1]` means the last position in *array*, `array[-2]` the next-to-last position, and so on.

An array can contain any type of values, including other arrays. In that case, you may need several indexing operators after each other:

```
array(array(int)) aai = ({
    ({ 7, 9, 8 }),
    ({ -4, 9 }),
    ({ 100, 1, 2, 4, 17 })
});
write("aai[2][3] is " + aai[2][3] + "\n");
```

This will print `aai[2][3] is 4`.

It is sometimes important to differentiate between two array expressions being **equal**, and two that also are the **same**. Whenever you write an array literal in your program, you get a new array. This array is only the **same** as itself, but it can be **equal** to other arrays. After executing the following code snippet, the variables a

Pike: an Introduction

and b will refer to the **same** array, but c will refer to an array that is just **equal** to the first one.

```
array(string) a = ({ "foo", "bar" });
array(string) b = a;
array(string) c = ({ "foo", "bar" });
```

If you compare them, *array1* == *array2* will be true if they are the *same* array:

```
a == b;   //this is true
a == c;   //this is false
```

equal(*array1*, *array2*) will also be true if they *look* the same:

```
equal(a, b);   //this is true
equal(a, c);   //this is also true
```

Here are some more of the many things that you can do with arrays:

- Check if it is an array

```
arrayp(something)
```

The function arrayp() returns **1** if the value *something* is an array, otherwise **0**.

- Extract a range

```
array[from..to]
```

returns a new array, containing the elements at the index *from* up to and including the index *to*.

({ 1, 7, 3, 3, 7 })[1..3] gives the result ({ 7, 3, 3 }).

The form `array[from..]` will give the elements starting at index `from` up to the end of the array. The form `array[..to]` will give the elements from the start of the array, up to and including index `to`.

- Concatenation

`array1 + array2`

returns a new array with the elements from both arrays, in the same order. This is a simple concatenation of the arrays, so duplicate elements are of course not removed.

`({ 7, 1, 1 }) + ({ 1, 3 })` gives the result `({ 7, 1, 1, 1, 3 })`.

- Union

`array1 | array2`

returns a new array with the elements that are present in `array1`, or in `array2`, or in both.

`({ 7, 1 }) | ({ 3, 1 })` gives the result `({ 7, 3, 1 })`.

- Intersection

`array1 & array2`

returns a new array with the elements that are present in both arrays.

`({ 7, 1 }) & ({ 3, 1 })` gives the result `({ 1 })`.

Pike: an Introduction

- Difference

    array1 - array2

returns a new array with the elements in the array `array1` that are not also present in the array `array2`.

`({ 7, 1 }) - ({ 3, 1 })` gives the result `({ 7 })`.

- Exclusive or

    array1 ^ array2

returns a new array with the elements that are present in *array1* or in array2, but not in both.

`({ 7, 1 }) ^ ({ 3, 1 })` gives the result `({ 7, 3 })`.

- Division

    array / delimiter

This will split the array *array* into an array of arrays. If *delimiter* is an array, the array *array* will be split at each occurrence of that array:

`({ 7, 1, 2, 3, 4, 1, 2, 1, 2, 77 }) / ({ 1, 2 })` gives the result `({ ({ 7 }), ({ 3, 4 }), ({ }), ({ 77 }) })`.

If *delimiter* is an integer, the array *array* will be split into arrays of size *delimiter*, with any extra elements ignored:

•

`({ 7, 1, 2, 3, 4, 1, 2 }) / 3` gives the result `({ ({ 7, 1, 2 }),`
`({ 3, 4, 1 }) })`.

If you convert the same integer to a floating-point number, the extra elements will not be thrown away:

`({ 7, 1, 2, 3, 4, 1, 2 }) / 3.0` gives the result `({ ({ 7, 1, 2 }),`
`({ 3, 4, 1 }), ({ 2 }) })`.

- Modulo

  `array % integer`

This gives the extra elements that would be ignored in the division operation `array / integer`:

`({ 7, 1, 2, 3, 4, 1, 2 }) % 3` gives the result `({ 2 })`.

- Finding the size

  `sizeof(array)`

returns the number of elements in the array *array*.

`sizeof( ({ }) )` gives the result **0**.

- Allocating an array with a number of elements

  `array a = allocate(size);`

Pike: an Introduction

This will create an array with *size* elements, where *size* is an integer. All the elements will have the value **0**.

- Reversing an array

```
reverse(array)
```

returns a new array with the elements in the array *array* in reverse order: with the first element last, and so on. This operation creates a copy, and does not change the array *array* itself.

- Finding an element in an array

```
search(haystack, needle)
```

returns the index of the first occurrence of an element equal to *needle* in the array *haystack*. If *needle* wasn't found, **-1** will be returned. The comparison is done with ==, so the element must be the same as the *needle*.

If only the existence of an element in an array is needed, the `has_value(haystack, needle)` can be used instead. It returns **1** on success and **0** on failure.

- Replacing elements in an array

```
replace(array, old, new)
```

replaces all the elements that are equal (with ==) to *old* with *new*. This operation does not create a copy, but changes the array *array* itself.

- Sorting an array

```
sort(array)
```

returns an array with all elements sorted.

The Data Type mapping

Mappings (also called dictionaries, hashes or associative arrays) let you translate from one value to another. This is possible since the mapping contains **index-value** pairs, consisting of two data items. If you know the **index**, Pike can quickly find the corresponding **value** for you.

A mapping literal can be written as a comma-separated list of index-value pairs inside parenthesis-square-bracket quotes:

```
([ "beer":"cerveza", "cat":"gato", "dog":"perro" ])
```

The data type of a mapping with indices of the type *index-type* and values of the type *value-type* is written mapping(*index-type*:*value-type*). The data type mapping(mixed:mixed) is a mapping that may contain any type of indices and values. It may also simply be written as mapping.

Here are a few variables that are mappings:

```
mapping(string:string) m;
mapping(int:float) mif = ([ 1:3.6, -19:73.0 ]);
mapping(string:string) english2spanish = ([
   "beer" : "cerveza",
   "cat" : "gato",
   "dog" : "perro"
```

Pike: an Introduction

```
]);
mapping(mixed:int) m2i = ([ 19.0 : 3, "foo" : 17 ]);
```

A mapping variable that hasn't been given a value contains **0**, and not an empty mapping. If you want an empty mapping, you have to assign it explicitly:

```
mapping(string:float) m1;  // m1 contains 0
m1 = ([ ]);    // Now m1 contains an empty mapping
mapping(int:int) m2 = ([ ]);
// m2 contains an empty mapping
```

When you want to **look** up a value in the mapping, you use the same **indexing operator** as for arrays: write the index within square brackets after the mapping. You may use this both to just retrieve values, and to change them:

```
write(english2spanish["cat"]); // Prints "gato"
english2spanish["dog"] = "gato";
    // Now, english2spanish["dog"] is "gato" too
english2spanish["beer"] = english2spanish["cat"];
    // Now, all values are "gato"
```

Index-value pairs may be inserted in the mapping either by writing them in the mapping literal, or with the indexing operator.

There is no specific order between the index-value pairs in a mapping, so there is no difference between the following two mapping literals:

```
([ 1:2, 3:4 ])
([ 3:4, 1:2 ])
```

If you try to look up an index that hasn't been inserted in the mapping, the index-ing operator will return **0**:

```
english2spanish["cat"]      // Gives "gato"
english2spanish["glurble"] // Gives 0
```

Lookups are done using ==, so the thing used as index in the lookup must be the **same** as the thing used when inserting things in the mapping. Remember that ar-rays, mappings and multisets may look the same, without being the same. Look at this example:

```
mapping(array(int) : int) m = ([ ]);
array(int) a = ({ 1, 2 });
m[a] = 3;
```

After running this code snippet, the expression m[a] will give the value **3**, but the expression m[({ 1, 2 })] will give the value **0**.

Mappings are similar to arrays. If you had a mapping from integers (to something), and used the integer values **0**, **1**, **2**, and so on, in order, this mapping would look much like an array. But mappings are more flexible, since you may use any type of values as indices.

Here are some useful things that you may do with mappings:

*   Check if it is a mapping

```
mappingp(something)
```

The function mappingp() returns **1** if the value *something* is a mapping, otherwise **0**.

Pike: an Introduction

- Comparing mappings

  ```
  mapping1 == mapping2
  ```

returns **1** if *mapping1* and *mapping2* are the same mapping, otherwise **0**. Just as with arrays, they have to be the same mapping, not just equal. You may also use the operator !=, which means "not the same".

- Comparing mappings (again)

  ```
  equal(mapping1, mapping2)
  ```

returns **1** if *mapping1* and *mapping2* have the same contents, otherwise **0**.

- Getting just the indices

  ```
  indices(mapping)
  ```

returns an array containing all the indices from the index-value pairs in the mapping *mapping*.

- Getting just the values

  ```
  values(mapping)
  ```

returns an array containing all the values from the index-value pairs in the mapping *mapping*. If you retrieve the indices (with indices()) and the values (with values()) from the same mapping, without performing any other mapping operations in between, the returned arrays will be in the same order. They may be be used as arguments to mkmapping() to create an equivalent copy of the mapping.

- Create a mapping

```
mkmapping(index-array, value-array)
```

builds a new mapping with indices from the array *index-array*, and the corresponding values from the array *value-array*.

- Union

```
mapping1 | mapping2
```

You may use **set operations** such as **union** (|) on mappings. All the indices in a mapping are considered as a set, and the set operators work with these sets. The values just "tag along".

The union operator returns a new mapping with the elements that are present in *mapping1*, or in *mapping2*, or in both. If an index is present in both mappings, the value part of the resulting index-value pair will come from the right-hand mapping (*mapping2*). Example:

```
([ 1:2, 3:4 ]) | ([ 3:5, 6:7 ])
```
gives the result ([1:2, 3:5, 6:7]).

Note that the elements in a mapping don't have a specified order.

The **addition operator** (+) to add two mappings together will give the same result as using **union** (|) because a mapping may only contain any index once, so when you try to "append" a mapping to another, any double indices will need to be removed.

Pike: an Introduction

- Intersection

  ```
  mapping1 & mapping2
  ```

returns a new mapping with the elements that are present in both mappings. The value parts of the resulting index-value pairs will come from the right-hand mapping (*mapping2*).

([1:2, 3:4]) & ([3:5, 6:7]) gives the result ([3:5]).

- Difference

  ```
  mapping1 - mapping2
  ```

returns a new mapping with the elements in the mapping *mapping1* that are not also present in the mapping *mapping2*.

([1:2, 3:4]) - ([3:5, 6:7]) gives the result ([1:2]).

- Exclusive or

  ```
  mapping1 ^ mapping2
  ```

returns a new mapping with the elements that are present in *mapping1* or in *mapping2*, but not in both.

([1:2, 3:4]) ^ ([3:5, 6:7]) gives the result ([1:2, 6:7]).

- Finding the size

  ```
  sizeof(mapping)
  ```

returns the number of index-value pairs in the mapping *mapping*.

`sizeof( ([ ]) )` gives the result **0**.

- Finding a value in a mapping

  `search(haystack, needle)`

This is a "reverse lookup" that searches among the values of the index-value pairs instead of among the indices. It returns the index of the index-value pair that has the value *needle* in the mapping *haystack*. If there are several index-value pairs that have the same *needle* as *value*, any of them may be chosen. The comparison is done with ==, so the element must be the same as the *needle*. Example:

`search(([ 1:2, 3:4, 4:5, 7:4 ]), 4)` gives either **3** or **7**.

- Replacing values in an mapping

  `replace(mapping, old, new)`

replaces all the values in mapping *mapping* that are equal (with ==) to *old* with *new*. This operation does not create a copy, but changes the mapping *mapping* itself. Example:

`replace(([ 1:2, 2:3, 3:2 ]), 2, 17)` gives the result `([ 1:17, 2:3, 3:17 ])`.

- Checking if an index is present

  `zero_type(mapping[index])`

returns **0** if the index *index* is present in the mapping *mapping*, otherwise it returns true. This may be useful to discriminate between an index that isn't present in the mapping, and one that is present but associated with the value **0**:

```
if(temp["sauna"] == 0)

{

  if(zero_type(temp["sauna"]))

    write("We don't know the temp in the sauna.\n");

  else

    write("It's mighty cold in that sauna.\n");

}
```

• Removing an index

```
m_delete(mapping, index)
```

will remove the index from the mapping, so that `zero_type(mapping[index])` will return true.

The Data Type multiset

A **set** is a container where a value is either a member or not. A **multiset** is a set where a value may be a member several times. It is just like a bag, where the contents don't have any particular order.

A multiset literal may be written as a comma-separated list of the elements, inside `(< >)` like this:

```
(< "foo", "bar", "fum", "foo", "foo" >)
```

The data type of a set with elements of the type *element-type* is written `multi-set(element-type)`. The data type `multiset(mixed)`, which is a multiset that may contain any type of elements, may also simply be written as `multiset`.

Other Reference Types

This section describes the following datatypes in greater depth than was previously provided:

functions or methods (`function`)

program or "class" (`program`)

objects or "instances" of a class (`object`)

Just like the container types, these types are **reference types**: When a data item of a basic type is stored in a variable, it is not the data item itself that is stored, but a reference to it.

The Data Type program

The data type `program` in Pike is used to contain class definitions. Not the **source code** or program text, but the internal representation that Pike generates when it has read and compiled the source code.

Pike: an Introduction

As described above in the chapter about object-oriented programming, programs and classes are the same in Pike. Both an explicit class definition (that is, with the keyword `class`) and a source code file can be used to define a program or class.

Here are some useful things that you can do with programs:

- Check if it is a program

  `programp(something)`

The function `programp()` returns **1** if the value *something* is a program, otherwise it returns **0**.

- Cloning

  `program-name()` or `program-name(arguments)`

This creates a new object of the type *program-name*. If arguments are given, they are sent to the function `create()` in this program.

- Defining variables

  `program-name variable-name;`

This creates a new variable of the type *program-name*.

Read more about classes and objects in the chapter about object-oriented programming.

The Data Type object

In object-oriented programming, the data items that are instances (also called **clones**) of a class are called objects. The data type object is used to store such objects.

An object is an **instance** of any class. Usually you use the more specific data type object(*classname*), which means an object that is an instance of the class *classname*. Instead of object(*classname*) you may also write just *classname* , which is the recommended form.

Here are some useful things that you can do with objects:

- Check if it is an object

  objectp(*something*)

The function objectp() returns **1** if the value something is an object, otherwise **0** is returned.

- Create an object

  program-name()

or

  program-name(*arguments*)

This creates a new object of the type *program-name*. If *arguments* are given, they are sent to the function create() in the program.

Pike: an Introduction

- Destroy an object

  ```
  destruct(object)
  ```

This destroys the object *object*. All variables that contain references to this object will be set to **0**. If there is a function called destroy() in the object, that function will first be called.

Note that usually you don't need to explicitly destroy objects. Pike has automatic garbage collection, and when an object is no longer referenced from anywhere, which means that it can never be used again, it is destroyed automatically.

- Accessing a member

  ```
  object -> member-name
  ```

This is used to access the function or member variable called *member-name* in the object *object*. The following example calls the function data in the object web_page:

```
web_page->data()
```

Read more about classes and objects in the chapter about object-oriented programming.

The Data Type function

Functions in Pike are **first class objects.** That is, they may be stored in variables or passed around as arguments.

A function stored in a variable may be called just like a normal function:

```
function w = write;
w("Hello!\n");
```

As you can see, you get a function reference of the type `function` by just typing the function name, without the parentheses used in function calls.

Here are some useful things that you can do with function references:

- Check if it is a function reference

  `functionp(something)`

The function `functionp()` returns **1** if the value *something* is a function reference, otherwise **0**.

- Find the name of a function

  `function_name(function)`

returns a string with the name of the function *function*. Example:

`function_name(w)` gives the result "`write`".

- Create an anonymous function

  `lambda(parameter-list){ function-body }`

returns a function that can be passed as an argument or assigned to a variable. For example, in an earlier chapter we defined a function `write_one()` to be given as an argument to `map()`. That function could also be written using `lambda` directly in the place of the argument:

Pike: an Introduction

```
map(all_of_them,
    lambda(int x){ write("Number: " + x + "\n"); });
```

Exercises

1. Name the various Pike datatypes and give some examples of the type of data that can be stored in each.

2. Write a function that checks the type of value passed as an argument and prints the type to the screen.

3. Explore the functionality of the `floor`, `ceil` and `round` functions. How does their behavior differ?

Working with Strings

After you complete this chapter, you should be able to:

1. Format and analyze strings using `sprintf()` and `sscanf()`.

2. Be able to identify the appropriate operator for performing a given operation on strings.

Chances are good that just about any program you write will involve string manipulation. After integers, strings are probably the most commonly used data type. Luckily, one of Pikes strengths is the powerful built in tools for working with strings. In fact, some, such as operators applied to strings, are so useful that you'll wonder how you ever got by without them.

String Operations

Pike has a large number of operations that you can do with strings. Some of them are expressed with operators such as + and −, and some are expressed as functions that you call from your program. We will start by looking at the indexing operator, [], and then explore the rest of the operators.

Here is a list of some operators that you can use with strings.

- Comparing strings
  ```
  string1 == string2
  ```

Pike: an Introduction

returns **1** if *string1* and *string2* are the same string, otherwise **0**. Unlike the container types, strings that look exactly the same *are* the same string.

You can also use the operator !=, which means "not the same". The relational operators (<, >, etc) do work with strings. These operators will use lexical order, i. e. the same order that the strings would be listed in a dictionary, if that dictionary considered all the characters, including blanks etc.

For example, "`foo`" would be listed before "`fum`", and is therefore smaller. As another example, "`foo`" would be listed before "`foobar`".

- Concatenation

  `string1 + string2`

returns a new string with *string1* and *string2* concatenated.

"`Foo`" + "`Bar`" gives the result "`FooBar`".

- Remove substrings

  `string1 - string2`

returns a new string where all occurrences of *string2* have been removed from *string1*.

  "`FooBarFoofooFum`" - "`Foo`" gives the result "`BarfooFum`".

Mathematically inclined programmers may want to note that for strings, it is not (necessarily) true that a+b-b equals a.

- Concatenation of string literals

String literals, which are strings within double quotes that are written in a program, may be concatenated by just putting them after each other:

```
write("Hello" " " "world!" + "\n");
```

- Indexing a character

To access individual characters inside a string, you use the same indexing operator as for arrays:

string[position]

There is no data type for characters in Pike, so when you extract or insert a character in a string, you really work with the character code of that character. The character code is an integer. But you don't need to look up character codes in a table. You can use **character literals**, such as `'b'`. The character literal `'b'` will be translated internally in Pike to **98**, which happens to be the character code for the character **b** (or something else, if you use a different character set than ISO-8859-1, also known as ISO Latin 1.)

You can use negative indices, just as with arrays: `string[-1]` means the last character in the string *string*, `string[-2]` the next-to-last character, and so on.

- Taking a range

```
string[from..to]
```

Pike: an Introduction

returns a new string, containing the characters at the index `from` up to and including the index `to`.

> `"ABCDEFG"[1..3]` gives the result `"BCDE"`.

The form `string[from..]` will give the characters starting at index `from` up to the end of the string. The form `string[..to]` will give the characters from the start of the string, up to and including index `to`.

- Division
  `string / delimiter`

This will split the string string into an array of strings, using occurrences of the string *delimiter* as places to cut.

`"abcdfoofoo x" / "foo"` gives the result (`{ "abcd", "", " x" }`).

An alternative is to divide with an integer, which will split the string into strings of the length given by that integer. Extra characters are thrown away:

`"abcdfoofoo x" / 5` gives the result (`{ "abcdf", "oofoo" }`).

If you divide with the same value as a floating-point number, the extra characters will not be thrown away:

`"abcdfoofoo x" / 5.0` gives the result (`{ "abcdf", "oofoo", " x" })`.

- Modulo

  ```
  string % integer
  ```

This gives the extra characters that would be ignored in the division operation `string / integer`:

`"abcdfoofoo x" % 5` gives the result `" x"`.

- Multiplication

  ```
  array * delimiter
  string * integer
  ```

The first usage will create a new string by concatenating all the strings in the array *array*, with the string *delimiter* between them:

`({ "7", "1", "foo" }) * ":"` gives the result `"7:1:foo"`.

The second form will concatenate *string* with itself *integer* times.

The functions `sprintf()` and `sscanf()` will be presented in their own sections, below.

- Check if it is a string

  ```
  stringp(something)
  ```

The function `stringp()` returns **1** if the value *something* is a string, otherwise **0**.

Pike: an Introduction

- Finding the size

```
sizeof(string)
```

returns the length (that is, the number of characters) in *string*.

`sizeof("hi ho")` gives the result **5**. `sizeof("")` gives the result **0**.

- Reversing a string

```
reverse(string)
```

returns a new string with the characters in reverse order.

`reverse("foo")` gives the result `"oof"`.

- Replacing parts in a string

```
replace(string, old, new)
```

returns a new string where all occurrences of the string *old* have been replaced with the string *new*.

`replace("fooFOOfoo", "foo", "fum")` gives the result `"fumFOOfum"`.

- Converting to lower case

```
lower_case(string)
```

returns a new string where all upper-case characters in *string* have been turned to lower case:

lower_case("A Foo IS!") gives the result "a foo is!".

- Converting to upper case
  upper_case(*string*)

returns a new string where all lower-case characters in the string *string* have been turned to upper case:

upper_case("A Foo IS!") gives the result "A FOO IS!".

- Capitalizing
  String.capitalize(*string*)

If the first character in the string *string* is a lower-case character, it is converted to upper case:

String.capitalize("xyz-Foo") gives the result "Xyz-Foo".

- Finding a substring in a string
  search(*haystack*, *needle*)

returns the index of the start of the first occurrence of the string *needle* in the string *haystack*:

search("sortohum", "orto") gives the result 1.

If *needle* is not found in the string *haystack*, **-1** will be returned.

Pike: an Introduction

Composing Strings with sprintf()

C programmers are familiar with the functions `sprintf()` and `sscanf()`, which are used to respectively create and analyze strings according to format specifiers. Pike has its own versions of `sprintf()` and `sscanf()`, which are not surprisingly, similar to those in C.

`sprintf()` can be used to build a string according to a string using format specifiers, and a number of arguments. For example, if the variables x and y both contain the floating-point number **2.0**, the expression

```
sprintf("They are %.2f and %10.3f.", x, y);
```

would give the result

```
"They are 2.00 and      2.000."
```

The format string consists of characters that will be copied to the result. The "percent specifiers", which are contained in the string will be replaced by the subsequent arguments to `sprintf()`. For example, `%d` is used to mark an integer.

Here is a list of some of the more common format specifiers:

Specifier	Meaning
%d	An integer in normal decimal (that is, base-10) notation
%o	An integer in octal (base-8) notation
%x	An integer in lower-case hexadecimal (base-16) notation

Specifier	Meaning
%X	An integer in upper-case hexadecimal notation
%c	The character corresponding to a certain character code
%f	A floating-point number
%s	A string
%{format%}	repeatedly output elements of an array according to *format*
%%	The percent (%) character

There is a large number of modifiers that you can use to control the format of the output. You insert these modifiers between the percent sign and the format character. Here are some examples of the most useful ones:

Modifier	Meaning
%Nd	An integer right-justified in a field at least N characters wide
%-Nd	An integer left-justified in a field at least N characters wide
%.Nf	A floating-point number printed with N decimals

Pike: an Introduction

Modifier	Meaning
%Nf	A floating-point number right-justified in a field at least N characters wide
%-N.Mf	A floating-point number with M decimals, left-justified in a field at least N characters wide
%-Ns	A string left-justified in a field at least N characters wide
%.Ms	A string, but at most M characters of that string are printed

C programmers should note that unlike the `sprintf()` in C, Pike's `sprintf()` returns the new string as the value of the call.

Analyzing strings with sscanf()

The counterpart or "opposite" of `sprintf()` is `sscanf()`. It looks at a string, and extracts values from it according to another string with format specifiers. It then places the values it has extracted in its arguments. The arguments must be variables, or other things that you can assign values to. For example, after the following code segment, the variable f will contain **-3.6**, and the variable i will contain **17**:

```
float f;
int i;
string the_string = "foo -3.6 fum dum 17";
```

```
sscanf(the_string, "foo %f fum dum %d", f, i);
```

Note that sscanf() isn't an ordinary built-in function, but a very special construction in Pike. The reason is that sscanf() has to change its arguments, and since Pike uses call-by-value, no ordinary function can do that. There is also a version of sscanf() that is an ordinary function: array_sscanf(). It returns all values it finds in an array. Apart from the way the values are returned, sscanf() and array_sscanf() behave identically.

The format string consists of characters, that should match the contents of the first string exactly. Blanks are significant. For example, the part " fum dum " in the format string must match a part of the analyzed string the_string exactly. The "percent specifiers" in the format string then match various things. For example, %d is used to match an integer.

Here is a list of format specifiers:

Specifier	Meaning
%d	An integer in normal decimal (that is, base-10) notation.
%o	An integer in octal (base-8) notation.
%x	An integer in hexadecimal (base-16) notation.

Pike: an Introduction

Specifier	Meaning
%D	An integer in decimal, or (if it starts with 0) octal, or (if it starts with 0x) hexadecimal notation. Hence, sscanf("12", "%D", i), sscanf("014", "%D", i) and sscanf("0xC", "%D", i) all yield the value **12** in i.
%f	A floating-point number.
%c	The character code of a single character.
%s	A string. If %s is followed by %d, %s will read any non-numerical characters. If followed by %[], %s will read any characters not present in the set in %[]. If followed by normal text, %s will match all characters up to, but not including, the first occurrence of that text.
%Ns	As above, but a string of exactly N characters
%[charac-ters]	A string containing any of the characters in the list *characters*. A minus sign can be used to give a range of values: %[a-d] means a string consisting of any of the characters a, b, c and d. A ^ sign means "not", so for example, %[^abc] means any character except a, b and c. They can be combined, so %[a-cf] means a, b, c, and f.

Specifier	Meaning
`%{format%}`	Repeatedly matches the format specifier *format* as many times as possible, and gives an array of arrays with the results. Example: `%{%d%}` matches zero or more integers.
`%%`	A single percent (`%`) character

If an asterisk (`*`) is put between the percent and the operator, e. g. `%*d`, the operator will only match its argument, and not assign any variables.

`sscanf()` returns the number of percent specifiers that were successfully matched.

The matching done by `sscanf()` is rather simple-minded. It looks at the format string up to the next `%`, and tries to match that with the analyzed string. If successful, it then goes on to the next part of the format string. If a part of the format string does not match, `sscanf()` immediately returns (with the number of percent specifiers that were successfully matched). Variables in the argument list that correspond to percent specifiers that were not successfully matched will not be changed.

Some examples of `sscanf()`:

```
sscanf("foo", "f%s", a);
```

This call to `sscanf()` will return **1**, and the variable a will be given the value "oo".

Pike: an Introduction

```
sscanf("4711bar", "%d%s", a, b);
```

The return value from this `sscanf()` statement will be **2**. a will be given the value **4711**. b will be given the value "`bar`".

```
sscanf(" \t test", "%*[ \t]%s", a)
```

The return value from `sscanf()` will be **1**, a will be given the value "`test`".

```
sscanf(str, "the %s", str);
```

This removes "`the `" from the beginning of the string in `str`. If `str` does not begin with "`the `", it will not be changed.

```
sscanf("foo % 1 2 3 fum", "%s %% %{%d%} %s", s1, a, s2);
```

This assigns "`foo`" to s1 and "`fum`" to s2, and the array (`{ ({ 1 })`, `({ 2 }), ({ 3 }) })` to a. The return value will be **3**.

```
sscanf("foo % 1 2 3 fum", "%s %% %{%d%} %s", string s1,
array(int) a, string s2);
```

A useful feature of `sscanf()` is that you can define variables inside it

In contrast to variables defined in a `for` statement, these variables are available in the rest of the block, and not just inside of `sscanf()`.

Wide strings

Normal strings contain characters with character codes between 0 and 255, also known as 8-bit characters. But Pike can also handle strings with characters with higher character codes. This is needed for some languages, such as Japanese. Such strings are called **wide strings**:

```
"The character \x123456 is the same as \d1193046."
```

This string contains two occurrences of the character with (decimal) character code 1193046. As you may remember, Pike will translate \x followed by a hexadecimal (that is, base 16) number in a string literal to the character with that character code. The same is true for \d followed by a decimal (that is, normal base 10) number, and for \ followed by an octal (base 8) number.

Internally, Pike will handle wide strings differently from normal 8-bit strings, but as a Pike programmer, you will usually not need to worry about the difference. Just use the characters you need. There may however be some operations, for example certain functions in certain modules, that cannot handle wide strings and only work with 8-bit strings.

Here are some functions that can be used to work with wide strings:

* `String.width(string data)`

This gives the width of the string *data*. This width of a string is the number of bits that is used to store each character in the string. Normal strings are 8 bits wide, but strings can also be 16 or 32 bits wide. For each string, Pike will use as few bits as possible. For example, "foo" will be 8 bits wide, "foo\d255" is also 8 bits wide, "foo\d256" is 16 bits wide, and "foo\d70000" is 32 bits wide.

* `string_to_utf8(string data)`

Pike: an Introduction

This translates the string *data*, which can be a wide string, to a string in the format UTF8. **UTF8** is a format that encodes wide characters in an 8-bit string.

- `utf8_to_string(string utf8_encoded_data)`

This translates an UTF8-encoded string *utf8_encoded_data* (which, due to the nature of the coding, can not be a wide string, since the UTF8 encoding is 8-bit by definition), to a Pike string.

The `Unicode` and `Locale` modules also contain functions that can be useful when working with wide strings.

Exercises

1. Using interactive Pike, experiment with applying the various "arithmetic" operations to strings.

2. Write a program that accepts user input and replaces spaces with underscores and removes punctuation marks.

3. Using interactive Pike, prepare statements using `sprintf` that perform the following:

   a. print a `float` with 2 fixed decimal places

   b. print an `int` in a field 5 characters wide, and include leading zeros (as in 09574).

c. print an `int` as a field of 4 "chars".

d. prints a string and an integer in the same function call.

e. prints the "debug" representation of any value.

4. Use interactive Pike to write `sscanf` statements that perform the following:

   a. read a `float` from a `string`.

   b. read an integer and a string separated by a space into an `int` and `string` variable, respectively.

   c. converts a string containing 4 characters into an integer.

   d. reads the first sentence of a paragraph into a string.

   e. reads a series of words separated by spaces into an array.

5. Experiment with wide strings by converting strings containing wide characters to UTF8 and vice versa.

Expressions and Operators

At the end of this chapter, you should be able to:

1. Name a few operators, and how they behave when applied to various datatypes.

2. Explain why operator precedence and associativity is important.

3. Explain how using parentheses can make it easier to understand and predict how an expression will be evaluated.

4. Describe the various methods for indexing, and explain what an "indexing error" is.

You'd be hard pressed to write a program that didn't use expressions or operators, but knowing what each is, and what it is used for, is important to writing better programs. Pike provides a wide range of expression syntaxes and operators. As we've seen in the previous chapter, many operators we normally associate with numeric calculations are available for use with non-numeric datatypes as well.

In order to be as efficient as possible, and to avoid confusion when discussing things with other Pike users, let's define a few useful terms:

- An **operation** is something Pike does, such as adding two values.

- An **operator** is the symbol we use in a program to write the operation, such as the operator +.

Pike: an Introduction

- An **operand** is a thing that an operation is applied to. For example, in the expression 7 + a there are two operands: 7 and a.

- An **expression** is what you get when you combine operators and operands according to the grammar rules of the language.

In this chapter we will examine how expressions are written in Pike. We will look at all the operations that have their own operators.

Arithmetic Operations

Pike can do all the usual arithmetic operations: addition (which is expressed with the operator +), subtraction (–), multiplication (*), division (/), and also modulo (%). The modulo operation, sometimes called "remainder" or "rest", gives the remainder from a division. For example, if you divide 7 by 3, 3 goes in 7 two times. But there is a remainder of 1, and that is the result of the modulo operation.

Here is a table of the most common arithmetic operations:

Operation	Syntax	Result
Addition	a + b	the sum of a and b
Subtraction	a – b	b subtracted from a
Negation	– a	minus a

Operation	Syntax	Result
Multiplica-tion	a * b	a multiplied by b
Division	a / b	a divided by b
Modulo	a % b	the remainder of a division between a and b

Remember that Pike makes a difference between numerical values that are integers (the type int), and numerical values that are real or "floating-point" numbers (the type float). This has some importance for how expressions with arithmetic operations are calculated by Pike. If at least one of the operands is a float, we use the floating-point versions of the operation. In if both operands are integers, we use a special integer-only version of the operation. For most of the operations, the only difference is that the type of the result will be different: 2 + 2 will give the integer value **4**, while 2 + 2.0 will give the floating-point value **4.0**. These differences become more critical when performing division.

When performing **floating-point division**, such as 9.0 / 4.0, the result is a floating-point value, in this case **2.25**. But with **integer division**, such as in 9 / 4, the result is only the integer part, in this case **2**.

The fact that integer division only gives the integer part can be treacherous: If 73 out of 92 people payed their income tax on time, don't try to calculate the percentage with the expression 73 / 92 * 100. That would give the result **0**.

Pike: an Introduction

Incrementing and Decrementing

It is very common in programs to increment or decrement a variable by one, such as in the statements

```
i = i + 1;
p = p - 1;
```

To simplify such programs, Pike has these extra operators:

Operation	Syntax	Result
Increment	++ a	increments a and returns the new value for a
Decrement	-- a	decrements a and returns the new value for a
Post increment	a ++	increments a and returns the old value for a
Post decrement	a --	decrements a and returns the old value for a

The two versions of increment, ++i and i++, both increment the value in the variable i with 1. The difference is if we want to use them as parts of a larger expression. In that case, ++i gives the new, incremented, contents of i as its value, while i++ gives the old contents of i as its value. The same difference applies to --i and i--.

The same operators used for arithmetical operations can also be used on some other data types. For example, by "adding" two arrays, you can concatenate them:

`({ 7, 6, 3 }) + ({ 6, 19 })` gives the result `({ 7, 6, 3, 6, 19 })`. These operations will be discussed later in this chapter.

Operations on Mixed Types

Here is a table of the results of the most common arithmetic operations with values of the various types in Pike:

Operation	Returned type	Result
`int + int`	`int`	The sum of the two values

`float + int`
`int + float`
`float + float`
	`float`	The sum of the two values

`string + string`
`int + string`
`float + string`
`string + int`
`string + float`
	`string`	In this case, any int or float is first converted to a string. Then the two strings are concatenated and the resulting string is returned.

`array + array`	`array`	The two arrays are concatenated into a new array and that new array is returned.

Pike: an Introduction

Operation	Returned type	Result
mapping + mapping	mapping	A mapping with all the index-value pairs from both mappings is returned. If an index is present in both mappings the index-value pair from the right mapping will be used.
multiset + multiset	multiset	A multiset with all the members from both multisets is returned.
int - int	int	The right value subtracted from the left.
float - int int - float float - float	float	The right value subtracted from the left.
string - string	string	A copy of the left string with all occurrences of the right string removed.
array - array	array	A copy of the right array with all elements present in the right array removed. Example: ({2,4,5,3,6,7}) - ({3,5}) will return ({2,4,6,7}).

Operation	Returned type	Result
mapping - mapping	mapping	A new mapping with all index-value pairs from the left mapping, except those indexes that are also present in the right mapping.
multiset - multiset	multiset	A copy of the left multiset without any member present in the left multiset.
- int	int	Same as 0 - *int*.
- float	float	Same as 0 – *float*.
int * int	int	The product of the two values
float * int int * float float * float	float	The product of the two values
array(string) * string	string	All the strings in the array are concatenated with the string on the right in between each string. Example: ({"foo","bar"})*"-" will return "foo-bar".

Pike: an Introduction

Operation	Returned type	Result
`int / int`	`int`	The right integer divided by the left integer rounded towards the next lower integer.

`float / int`
`int / float`
`float / float`
	`float`	The right value divided by the left value.

`string / string`	`array(string)`	In symmetry with the multiplication operator, the division operator can split a string into pieces. The right string will be split at every occurrence of the right string and an array containing the results will be returned. Example: `"foo-bar"/"-"` will return `({"foo","bar"})`
`int % int`	`int`	The rest of an integer division.

`float % float`
`int % float`
`float % int`
	`float`	The rest of a division.

Comparison Operators

Pike lets you compare things to each other.

Operation	Syntax	Result
Same	a == b	**1** if a is the same as b, **0** otherwise
Not same	a != b	**0** if a is the same as b, **1** otherwise
Greater than	a > b	**1** if a is greater than b, **0** otherwise
Greater than or equal to	a >= b	**1** if a is greater to or equal to b, **0** otherwise
Lesser than	a < b	**1** if a is less than b, **0** otherwise
Lesser than or equal to	a <= b	**1** if a is less than or equal to b, **0** otherwise

As you may remember, Pike interprets the value zero (**0**) as **false**, and everything else is interpreted as **true**. The comparison operators give a truth value as result, and to simplify things they always return **0** for **false** and **1** for **true**.

The operators == and != can be used on any type. Note that these two operators check if two things are the same, not just if they are equal. For two things to be the same, first of all they have to have the same type. For example, **1** and **1.0** may be equal, but they are not the same.

Pike: an Introduction

All values of the basic types (integers, floating-point values, and strings) that are of the same type and that are equal, are also the same. The expressions 7 == 7 and "hi" == "hi" will always be **true**. With the other types, the so-called reference types, it is more difficult: Two arrays can have the same length and contain the same elements, but still be two separate arrays. For a comparison like a1 == a2 to be true, where a1 and a2 are array variables, they must refer to the same array, not just two similar arrays. (See also the section "The difference between basic types and reference types" in the chapter about data types.)

To check if two things are similar, even if they are not necessarily the same, you can use the function equal(). This comparison will be true:

```
equal( ({ 7, 1, ({ 7 }) }), ({ 7, 1, ({ 7 }) }) )
```

but this one will be false:

```
({ 7, 1, ({ 7 }) }) == ({ 7, 1, ({ 7 }) })
```

The relational operators >, >=, <, and <= can only be used with integers, floating-point values, and strings. If you compare an integer with a floating-point value, the integer will be converted to a floating-point value before the comparison.

When comparing strings, lexical or "alphabetical" order is used. Different countries sort their alphabets in different order, and if your operating system supports this, Pike will too. For example, in Unix you can set the environment variables LC_CTYPE and LC_LANG, and Pike will use their values to determine the right sorting order.

Logical Expressions

We often want to express conditions such as "if this is true, and that is true, then we do something". Such calculations with **truth values** are done with the logical operators in Pike:

Operation	Syntax	Result
Logical and	a && b	If a is **false**, a is returned and b is not evaluated. Otherwise, b is returned.
Logical or	a || b	If a is **true**, a is returned and b is not evaluated. Otherwise, b is returned.
Logical not	! a	Returns **0** if a is **true**, **1** otherwise.

For example, if the temperature is below 100 degrees, and we still have some fuel, we want to burn some more:

```
if(temperature < 100 && fuel > 0)
  burn();
```

Both && and || always calculate their first argument, but the second one is calculated only if it is necessary to find the value of the entire expression. In a && b, if a is false, a and b can never be true, so we don't bother to calculate b. This is useful in cases like this:

```
if(i < sizeof(a) && a[i] != 0)
smorgle(a);
```

Pike: an Introduction

If i is too big to be a valid index in the array a, which we check in the first part of the condition, we will get an error if we try the operation a[i], and our program will be interrupted.

Since the || operator returns the first argument that is non-zero, there is a useful trick that can be used to check a number of variables:

```
return a || b || "";
```

This will return a, except in the case when a is **0**, in which case it will return b. Except in the case when b also is **0**, in which case it will return an empty string.

Bitwise and Set Operations

In the rare cases where you have to fiddle with the bits inside integers, you can use the bitwise operations in Pike. They work just like in C and C++, and if you need to use them, you probably already know what they mean.

Operation	Syntax
Shift left	a << b
Shift right	a >> b
Bitwise not	~ a
Bitwise and	a & b
Bitwise or	a | b

Operation	Syntax
Bitwise exclusive or	a ^ b

Some of the operators that are used for bitwise operations (| , - , & , and ^) can also be used for operations on sets, such as union and intersection. They can be applied not only to multisets, but also to arrays and mappings.

Operation	Syntax	Result
Intersection (and)	a & b	All elements present in both a and b.
Union (or)	a | b	All elements present in at least one of a and b.
Symmetric difference (exclusive or)	a ^ b	All elements present in a or b, but not present in both.
Difference	a - b	All elements present in a, but not in b.

When using mappings in set operations, we only consider the indices. The values are copied along with the indices. If an index is present in both mappings in a union or intersection, the one from the right-side mapping will be used. Some examples:

```
mapping m1 = ([ 1:"one", 2:"two" ]),
```

Pike: an Introduction

```
m2 = ([ 2:"TWO", 3:"THREE" ]);
```

Expression	Result
m1 & m2	([2:"TWO"])
m1 | m2	([1:"one", 2:"TWO", 3:"THREE"])
m1 + m2	([1:"one", 2:"TWO", 3:"THREE"])
m1 ^ m2	([1:"one", 3:"THREE"])
m1 - m2	([1:"one"])

For & and – the value on the right side may also be an array or a multiset. In these situations, the array or multiset will be taken as the set of indexes to operate with, as if a mapping had been provided.

You can also use the operator + on arrays and mappings. For mappings, it calculates the union, i.e. the same as the | operator. For arrays, it gives a different result: it just concatenates the arrays, instead of calculating the union:

Expression	Result
({ 1, 2, 4 }) | ({ 3, 4 })	({ 1, 2, 3, 4 })

Expression	Result
`({ 1, 2, 4 }) + ({ 3, 4 })`	`({ 1, 2, 4, 3, 4 })`

Indexing

The data items of some of the data types in Pike can contain other data items. The indexing and range operators are used to retrieve information from inside those complex data items.

Operation	Syntax	Result
Indexing	`a [ b ]`	The value at index or position b in a
Assign at index	`a [ b ] = c`	Sets the value at index or position **b** in a to c
Range	`a [ b .. c]`	Returns a slice of a, i. e. the elements in a starting at the index b and ending at c

Pike: an Introduction

Operation	Syntax	Result
Range	`a [ .. c]`	Returns a slice of a, starting at the beginning of a and ending at *c*
Range	`a [ b .. ]`	Returns a slice of a, from the index *b* to the end of a

Note that the indices in an array start with 0, so the last index value in an array is equal to the length of the array minus one.

You may remember the syntax for accessing functions and member variables in an object, using the operator `->`. This is actually a form of indexing, and the `->` operator is just a different way of writing the indexing operator. If you turn the identifier in the expression `something->identifier` into a string by putting double quotes around it, you can use the `[]` indexing operators, like this:

Operation	Syntax	Result
Indexing	`a->identifier`	Equivalent to a`["identifier"]`
Assign at index	`a->identifier=c`	Equivalent to a`["identifier"]=c`

Because an identifier can only contain alphanumeric characters and underscores, the `[]` indexing syntax is also useful when you want to index a mapping, object or multiset with a value that contains spaces or other charaters. You can index strings, arrays, mapping, multisets and objects. Some of these can only be indexed with certain types of index values, as shown in this list:

Operation	Returns
string[int]	Returns the numerical value of a character in the string. The result is not a character or a string, but just the integer used internally to represent the character. To get a single character string, use string[int..int]. Note that the first character has index number 0, and so on.
array[int]	Returns an element in the array
array[int]=mixed	Sets an element in the array to the mixed value.
multiset[mixed] multiset->identifier	Returns **1** if the index (the value between the brackets) is a member in the multiset, **0** otherwise.
multiset[mixed]=mixed multiset->identifier=mixed	If the rightmost *mixed* value is **true**, the index value is added as a member to the multiset. Otherwise it is removed once from the multiset.

Pike: an Introduction

Operation	Returns
`mapping[mixed]` `mapping->identifier`	Returns the value associated with the index, or **0** if it is not found. Note that 0 may also mean that the index exists, but its value is 0. To verify that an index does not exist, use `zero_type(mapping[mixed])`.
`mapping[mixed]=mixed` `mapping->identifier=mixed`	Associate the second mixed value with the first mixed value.
`object[string]` `object->identifier`	Returns the value of the variable that is named by the identifier in the object.
`object[string]=mixed` `object->identifier=mixed`	Set the given identifier in the object to the mixed value. Only works if the identifier references a variable in the object that isn't restricted by an access control keyword.
`string[int..int]`	Returns a piece of the string.
`array[int..int]`	Returns a slice of the array.

When indexing an array or string, it is sometimes convenient to start counting from the end instead of from the beginning. You can do this with negative indices.

The last element in the array can be accessed with index -1, the second-to-last element with index -2, and so on. In general, `arr[-i]` is equivalent to `arr[sizeof(arr)-i]`.

Note that negative indices do not work with the range operator (as opposed to the index operator.) If you pass a negative index to the range operator, they will be converted to zero (0).

Assignment Type Conversions

Assignment is used to give a new value to a variable:

```
i = 16;
i = i + 15;
```

"Variable" is used in a general sense here. Assignment can give values not only to normal variables, but also to member variables in an object, and to positions within an array, a mapping or a multiset:

```
my_cat->name = "Schrödinger";
a[7] = 8;
english2german["four"] = "vier";
set_of_winners["Tom"] = 0;
```

An assignment, such as k = 3, is an expression, and its value is the same value as was assigned to the variable. You can use an assignment expression within another expression, for example in a "chain" of assignments that assign the same value to several variables:

```
i = j = k = 3;
```

Pike: an Introduction

Pike includes some "shortcuts" designed to make coding easier and to cut down on possible mistakes. The heart of these shortcuts is the notion that assignments that follow the pattern

```
i = i + 3;
k = k * 4;
miles_traveled["Anne"] = miles_traveled["Anne"] + 5;
debt[get_name()] = debt[get_name()] + 500;
```

are very common in programming. That is, an assignment to a variable, where you use the old value of the variable to calculate the new one. To simplify such assignments, Pike has a number of extra assignment operators, which look like *operator=*, for example:

```
i += 3;
k *= 4;
miles_traveled["Anne"] += 5;
debt[get_name()] += 500;
```

The expression

```
variable operator= expression
```

means the same as

```
variable = variable operator expression
```

But note that the variable part is only calculated once. For example, in

```
debt[get_name()] += 500;
```

the function get_name() is only called one time.

Syntax	Equivalent to
variable += expression	variable = variable + expression
variable -= expression	variable = variable - expression
variable *= expression	variable = variable * expression
variable /= expression	variable = variable / expression
variable %= expression	variable = variable % expression
variable <<= expression	variable = variable << expression
variable >>= expression	variable = variable >> expression
variable |= expression	variable = variable | expression
variable &= expression	variable = variable & expression
variable ^= expression	variable = variable ^ expression

Note that the increment and decrement operators (i++, ++i, i--, and --i) also change the value of the variable they are used on.

Pike: an Introduction

Multi-Assignment

In Pike, you can assign values to several variable at once, taking the values from an array, surrounding the assignees with square brackets [and]:

```
int i;
string s;
float f1, f2;
[i, s, f1, f2] = ({ 3, "hi", 2.2, 3.14 });
```

This syntax is very convenient when you deal with functions which always return a fixed-width array of data.

Type Conversions

Values of one type can be converted to a value of another type. For example, the integer 4711 can be converted to the string "4711". These two may look similar, but they are actually entirely different things. For example, 4711 + 3 will give you 4714, "4711" + "3" will give you "47113". We call the process of converting a value from one type to another **value casting**, that is, we "**cast**" a value from one type to another.

Some conversions are done automatically. For example, in the expression "hello" + 17 the integer 17 will be automatically converted to the string "17", before the two strings are concatenated, giving the result "hello17". But some conversions need to be performed with a special operation, called an explicit type conversion or cast. There is a special cast operator, which is written as a data type between parentheses:

```
(float)14    // Gives the float 14.0
```

```
(int)6.9     // Gives the int 6

(string)6.7  // Gives the string "6.7"

(float)"6.7" // Gives the float 6.7

(array)"6.7" // Gives the array ({54, 46, 55})

(array(int))({14.0, 6.9, 6.7}) // Gives the array ({14, 6, 6})
```

Here is a list of some useful casts:

Casting from	to	gives the result
int	float	The floating-point number with the same value as the integer
float	int	An integer, with the fractional part ("the decimals") just skipped
int	string	Converts the integer to a string with a number in normal base-10 notation
float	string	Converts the floating-point number to a string
string	int	Converts the first number in the string to an integer. The number should be an integer written in normal base-10 notation.
string	float	Converts the first number, with or without decimals, in the string to a floating-point number

Pike: an Introduction

Casting from	to	gives the result
string	program	If the string contains a filename, compile the file and return the program. The results are cached.
string	array	Converts a string into an array containing the integer value of each character in the string.
string	object	First casts the string to a program as above, and then clones the result. The results are cached.
array	array(*type*)	This casts all values in the array to type.
mapping	array	This creates a twodimensional array of index/value pairs.
multiset	array	The same as doing indices(*multiset*).

Type Casting and type assertion

Sometimes you know more about data types than Pike does, and you want to tell Pike what you know. For example, let's say that you have a variable with the type mixed, which means that it can contain any type of data. Let's also say that you happen to know that that variable contains an integer. If you want to use this value where an integer is required, Pike might complain about it:

```
mixed m;

int i;

m = 18;

i = m;  // This will make Pike suspicious and produce a
warning
```

You can use a **type (or soft) cast** to tell Pike that m is an integer and nothing else:

```
i = [int]m; // Don't worry. I promise it's an int!
```

Note that this form of casting will not change the type of m. If m contains a string, Pike will happily assign it to i without complaints. Pike won't find out that there was a problem until it tries to use the value of i and finds out it's really a string instead of an integer. Also, you should be aware that the term "type cast" has a slightly different meaning in Pike compared to other languages, where it more closely resembles Pike's "value cast".

Soft casting is useful when you are running Pike in its strict_types mode. In this situation, you can use soft casts to tell the compiler that your code will ensure that the right types are passed in your code:

```
int foo(int a)

{

return a+1;

}

int main()

{
```

```
   mixed a = 1;
   if(intp(a))
// we know that a will be an integer, even though it
// could really be anything.
      return foo([int]a);
   else return 0;
}
```

The Comma Operator

The **comma** operator, written as a comma (,) takes two operands. It evaluates its left operand and discards the value. It then evaluates its right operand, and returns that value as the result of the expression.

```
7 + 3, 6 * 2 // Gives 12
3,14         // Gives 14 (and not pi)
```

The comma operator is seldom necessary, except in function-like preprocessor macros, which we advise against anyway.

The commas used to separate the arguments in a call to a function, or the elements in an array, are not comma operators.

Call, Splice and Automap

In this section we explain operators that are used in connection with functions: the **function-call** operator and the **splice** operator and arrays: the automap operator.

A function call, which we have seen many examples of, is actually a use of the function-call operator. It is written with a pair of parentheses according to this template:

```
function-expression ( argument-list )
```

First the *function-expression* is calculated, to find out which function to call. The *function-expression* is often a single identifier, such as `write`, but can be more complicated. Then all the expressions in the comma-separated *argument-list* are calculated. Finally, the function is executed, with the argument values as parameters.

Some notes about the function-call operator:

* If the value of the function-expression is an array, Pike assumes that each element in the array is a function that can be called. Pike will call each function in that array, with the given arguments, and the result of all this is an array with the return values from the calls.

* If the value of the function-expression is a program (that is, a class), Pike will create (or clone) a new object from that class, and then call the function create in that object, with the given arguments.

The **splice** operator, written with a commercial-at sign (@), allows us to use an array as an argument list. For example,

```
array a = ({ 17, -0.3, "foo" });
koogle(@a);
is equivalent to
koogle(17, -0.3, "foo");
```

Pike: an Introduction

The splice operator is useful when assembling arguments for calling a function when the arguments are highly variable.

The automap operator (`[*]`) is related to `map()` which calls a function repeatedly with each element of the array. `[*]` lets you apply each element of an array to the surrounding operation which can be much more flexible than using `map()`

```
array c = koogle(a[*]);
array d = a[*] + a[*];
array e = b[ ({2,4})[*] ];
```

is equivalent to

```
array c = map(a, koogle);
array d = map(a, lambda(mixed m){ return m+m; });
array e = map( ({2,4}), lambda(int i){ return b[i]; });
```

or

```
array c = ({ koogle(17), koogle(-0.3), koogle("foo") });
array d = ({ a[0]+a[0], a[1]+a[1], a[2]+a[2] });
array e = ({ b[2], b[4] });
```

The last example is of course not useful unless you know the array already, but it illustrates what is actually happening. `[*]` should be used judiciously as it can make code potentially hard to read.

The use of `()` on an array as described above is actually an implicit application of automap. This implicit use of automap to arrays also works with `->` and `[]` (when used with a non-integer values).

Operator Precedence and Associativity

Operator precedence is the reason why the expression 5 + 3 * 2 is calculated as 5 + (3 * 2), giving 11, and not as (5 + 3) * 2, giving 16.

The multiplication operator (*) has higher "precedence" or "priority" than the addition operator (+), so the multiplication must be performed first.

Operator associativity is why the expression 8 - 3 - 2 is calculated as (8 - 3) - 2, giving 3, and and not as 8 - (3 - 2), giving 7.

The subtraction operator (-) is "left associative", so the left subtraction must be performed first. When we can't decide by operator precedence alone in which order to calculate an expression, we must use associativity.

Since the operators + and - have the same precedence, and are left-associative, the following expressions are all equivalent:

```
x + 3 - y + 5
(x + 3) - y + 5
((x + 3) - y) + 5
```

Since the operators =, += and -= have the same precedence, and are right-associative, the following expressions are all equivalent:

```
x = y += z -= 4
x = y += (z -= 4)
x = (y += (z -= 4))
```

Pike: an Introduction

You can use parentheses to tell the compiler in which order to evaluate things. If you don't use parentheses, Pike will use the precedences and the associativities of the operators to decide in which order to perform them. Spaces have no effect.

This table shows the priority and associativity of each operator in Pike, with the highest priority at the top:

Operators	Associativity
`::a` `a::b`	left to right

`a()`
`a[b]`
`a->b`
`a[b..c]`
	left to right

`a++ a--`	left to right

`!a`
`~a`
`(type)a`
 	
`[type]a`
`++a`
`--a`
	right to left!

Operators	Associativity

`a*b`
`a/b`
`a%b`
	left to right

`a+b` `a-b`	left to right
`a>>b` `a<<b`	left to right

`a>b`
`a>=b`
`a<b`
`a<=b`
	left to right

`a==b  a!=b`	left to right
`a&b`	left to right
`a^b`	left to right
`a|b`	left to right
`a&&b`	left to right

Pike: an Introduction

Operators	Associativity
a||b	left to right
a?b:c	right to left!
a=b a+=b a-=b a*=b a/=b a%=b a<<=b a>>=b a&=b a|=b a^=b	right to left!
@a	right to left!
a,b	left to right

Examples:

This expression	is evaluated in this order
a+b*c	a+(b*c)

This expression	is evaluated in this order
a+b*c*d	a+((b*c)*d)
(a+b)*c*d	((a+b)*c)*d
a+d,c=b|c+e	(a+d),(c=(b|(c+e)))
a + e&d == c	(a + e) & (d == c)
c=1,99	(c=1),99
!a++ + ~f()	(!(a++)) + (~(f()))
a?b:c?d:e	a?b:(c?d:e)
s == "klas" || i < 9	(s == "klas") || (i < 9)
r = s == "sten"	r = (s == "sten")

All of this discussion about operator precedence might seem confusing and a bit overwhelming. It can certainly be the source of bugs and undesired program behavior. The recommended practice is to use parentheses in order to explicitly describe the order in which you wish to have operations performed. Using this technique, you can always be sure that operations are performed in the order you intend them to. It also makes reading program listings much simpler, as you don't have to spend time figuring out the operation order.

Pike: an Introduction

Exercises

1. Explore the various arithmetic operations on `float` and `int` values using interactive Pike.

2. Explore the various operations on non-numeric values using interactive Pike.

3. Explain how some of the following arithmetic expressions would be evaluated:

   a. `8 + 3 - 2`

   b. `4 + 2 * 7 / 9 -2`

   c. `int a = 2; 9 % 3 + a++`

   d. `(3 + 2) * 4 - 3`

4. Use interactive Pike to create a mapping that contains indices with non alphanumeric characters. Experiment using `->` and `[]` to try to retrieve values in the mapping.

The Preprocessor

When you complete this chapter, you should be able to:

1. Explain some of the preprocessor directives available.

2. Describe the dangers of using the preprocessor in your Pike code.

When Pike executes a program file, the source code is first run through the **preprocessor**, The preprocessor performs some textual transformations on the source code. By "textual transformations" we mean that the preprocessor doesn't know a lot about Pike, and just looks at the source code as text, where it for example can replace some of the words.

Note that we recommend that you don't use the preprocessor at all, unless you have to. Most of what the preprocessor can do, can be done in better ways in Pike. However, there are a few things where the preprocessor is useful, and since it is used by many, if not all, Pike programs, we will introduce its basic functionality here. Don't be surprised, however, if we try to discourage its use at every turn.

The preprocessor is controlled by **preprocessor directives**. A preprocessor directive must be written on its own line, and starts with a hash character (#). This is an example of a preprocessor directive:

```
#define MAX_TEMP 100
```

This directive defines the **macro** MAX_TEMP. The preprocessor will now replace the word MAX_TEMP with 100 in the rest of the file, before translating and executing the source code.

Pike: an Introduction

Pike will replace every occurrence of MAX_TEMP in the rest of the file with 100. You can imagine that this can cause trouble if you are not careful. It is better to use a real constant:

```
constant MAX_TEMP = 100;
```

Preprocessor macros can have arguments:

```
#define square(x) x * x
```

This define directive will cause the Pike preprocessor to replace every occurrence of "square(expression)" in the file with "expression * expression". Note, however, that this is just a textual transformation! As an example of what this means, the statement

```
i = square(2 + 3);
```

which we expect to assign 25 to the variable i, will be translated to

```
i = 2 + 3 * 2 + 3;
```

where multiplication, as always, has higher precedence than addition. The result is that a value of 11 will be assigned to i. Macros have several other problems similar to this one, so whenever you can you should use a function instead:

```
int square(int x) { return x * x; }
```

Another unfortunately common preprocessor directive is the **include** directive:

```
#include "somefile.pike"
```

Before the source code is translated, this directive will be replaced by the contents of the file "somefile.pike". By including another Pike file, we can implement a primitive form of inheritance. If that is what you are doing, it is much better to use the real inheritance mechanism:

```
inherit "somefile.pike";
```

Other useful preprocessor directives include:

```
#charset <charset-name>
```

Tell Pike which character set you are using in the Pike source code. The default character set is iso8859-1, which is the correct set for English and most Western European languages. Some other character sets are utf-8 and iso2022.

```
string multi = #"multi \"line\"
text";
```

set a string with linebreaks. Escapes with \ are still applied.

```
string file = #string "filename";
```

read the contents of "filename" into a string. This is equivalent to

```
string file = Stdio.read_file("filename");
```

but is done before the code is compiled, while the latter is evaluated at runtime.

```
#pragma strict_types
```

do strict type checking at runtime. By default Pike does strict type checking only when the code is compiled, but not when it is run.

Pike: an Introduction

Magic Preprocessor Constants

The preprocessor also expands a few specific keywords to Pike constants (C programmers will feel right at home); a __LINE__ in your code will be translated to an integer pointing out at which line the keyword was found. __DATE__ will be expanded to a "Mon day Year" string constant, e g "May 2 2000"with the date when the file was compiled (or, more to the point, when the preprocessor replaced the entity). Similarly, __TIME__ turns into a 24-hour "HH:MM:SS" time string constant, e g "19:17:21".

Introduction to Modules

When you complete this chapter, you should be able to:

1. List some of the built-in Pike modules and the functionality available in them.

2. Explain the difference between a module and a class or program.

3. Write a simple Pike module.

A module is a sort of "plug-in": a software package that can easily be used by other programmers. Modules can contain functions, classes, constants, and also other modules. We will use the term **members** for something, such as a function, that a module contains. Some modules are written in Pike, but C and C++ can also be used.

Bundled Modules

Pike is delivered with a number of useful modules, and many more are available from various sources, including the Pike Module Repository. Here is a list of a few of the more interesting modules that are bundled with Pike.

*   `Stdio`

    This module is used for reading and writing files, and also for communication over the Internet, and for text-based dialogues with the user. We have used the **Stdio** module in several examples in this introduction.

Pike: an Introduction

- GTK

  A toolkit for creating graphical user interfaces, with windows, buttons and so on.

- Image

  Processing and manipulation of pictures.

- Protocols

  Various protocols, i. e. ways of communicating. One of these is `Protocols.HTTP`, which is used to communicate with World Wide Web servers in order to retrieve web pages. Some other supported protocols are **DNS**, **IMAP**, **IRC**, **LDAP**, **SMTP**, and **TELNET**.

- MIME

  Support for decoding and encoding emails using MIME, which is most notably used in electronic mail.

- Crypto

  Support for cryptography.

- Calendar

  Extensive support for various calendar and date calculations.

- `Sql`

  This module lets Pike use SQL database queries, with database servers such as mySQL, PostgreSQL, Oracle and Sybase.

- `Thread`

  Support for threaded execution of Pike programs.

- `Process`

  Functions to start and control other processes.

- `Getopt`

  Routines to interpret and handle command line options.

- `Gz`

  Support for unpacking compressed files.

- `Regexp`

  Support for matching regular expressions.

Depending on which operating system you are using, and on exactly how Pike was installed on your system, some of these modules may not be available.

Pike: an Introduction

How do you use a Module?

To use a member of a module, just prefix the member name with the module name and a dot (.). For example, we have already used the standard input, which is called `Stdio.stdin`. That means that it is the member `stdin` in the module `Stdio`. In this example, we read a string from the standard input by calling the function `gets()` in the object `Stdio.stdin`:

```
string name = Stdio.stdin->gets();
```

We have also used the class `Protocols.HTTP.Query`, which is the member `Query` in the module `Protocols.HTTP`. Note that the module `Protocols.HTTP` is actually the module `HTTP`, which is a member of the module `Protocols`. In this example, we use the class `Protocols.HTTP.Query` as the data type when defining a variable:

```
Protocols.HTTP.Query web_page;
```

If we don't want to write the module name every time we use something from that module, we can **import** the module.

```
import Stdio;
import Protocols.HTTP;
```

After **importing** those two modules, we can use both `stdin` and `Query` without prefixing them with anything:

```
string name = stdin->gets();
Query web_page;
```

Importing can be done anywhere in a program, but we usually do it at the top of the program.

If we import two modules that contain the same name, that name will refer to the module that was imported last. An example where the modules `canvas_window` and `chess_game` both contain the function `draw()`:

```
import canvas_window;
draw(); // Lets you draw pictures
import chess_game;
draw(); // A draw in a chess game: nobody wins
```

Even if you have imported a module, you can use the module name to determine which module you mean:

```
canvas_window.draw(); // Lets you draw pictures
```

You can import all the modules in a directory by giving the directory name as a string:

```
import "/home/blubbers/pike/all_my_modules";
import ".";
```

If you refer to a module with the module name prefixed by just a dot, Pike will look for the module in the same directory as the program that used the module:

```
import .florble;
.gnooble.droop(7, 3);
```

It's important to note that while using import can save you a good deal of typing, it does not make your program any faster, in fact Pike will search through all the imported modules to find a function. It also has the real potential to make your code difficult to follow, and can cause unintended behavior if you import two modules that have overlapping identifiers.

Pike: an Introduction

How do you create a new Module?

A module is a package of Pike code, typically a file. You can also write modules in C or C++, but how to do that is outside the scope of this introduction.

Let's say that we want to create a module called trig, which has two members: a function cos2() that calculates the square of the cosine function, and the constant pi.

We create a file, called trig.pmod, with the following contents:

```
float cos2(float f)
{
  return pow(cos(f), 2.0);
}
constant PI = 3.1415926535;
```

Now that the module file exists, we can use it. If we use it from a program that is stored in the same directory as trig.pmod, we can use the .module-name notation, so the program will look like this:

```
int main()
{
  write("The square of cos(pi/4) is " +
            .trig.cos2(.trig.PI/4) + ".\n");
  return 0;
}
```

Or, if we prefer to import the module:

```
import .trig; // Import the module from this directory
```

```
int main()

{

  write("The square of cos(pi/4) is " +

          cos2(PI/4) + ".\n");

  return 0;

}
```

How does Pike find the Modules?

Here is a somewhat detailed explanation of exactly how Pike finds the modules that you tell it to use. Normally you don't really need to worry about all the details, except for what is needed to put your own modules in a place where Pike can find them. But sometimes the details can be important, for example if there are several modules with the same name, but in different places, or if you want to do something advanced and ingenious with modules.

Every module that is used somewhere in your program is loaded when the program starts. It doesn't matter if you are importing the entire module, or if you are just using a "qualified" name such as smorglemod.fnordle() (that is, the function fnordle() in the module smorglemod). This is done even before main() is called. That the module is loaded means that the file is read from disk, and the things in the module are made accessible to your program.

When Pike loads a module with the name *module-name*, Pike will look for a module with that name in the following directories, in this order:

Pike: an Introduction

1. If the *module-name* was prefixed with a dot, in the same directory as the program that used the module, otherwise:

2. In directories that have been imported with import "*directory-name*".

3. In directories that were added with add_module_path() before the program that tries to load the module has been compiled.

4. In directories specified with -M on the command line.

5. In directories listed in the environment variable PIKE_MODULE_PATH.

6. In the directory with builtin modules, for example called /usr/local/pike/7.6.6/lib/modules/ or C:\Program Files\Pike\lib\pike\modules, depending on your operating system and the directory that it was configured to be installed into.

In each of those directories, Pike will look for files or subdirectories, in this order:

1. If there is a file called *module-name*.pmod, Pike will load that file as a Pike program, clone it, and use the newly-cloned object as a module.

2. If there is a directory called *module-name*.pmod, Pike will create a module that has all the modules in that directory as members. If there is a module called module (that is, with the file name module.pmod, module.pmod-.pike, or module.pmod.so) in the directory *module-name*.pmod, the members from that module will be used instead of the modules actually present in the directory.

3. If there is a file called *module-name*.pmod.pike, Pike will load that file as a Pike program, clone it, and use the newly-cloned object as a module. Note that this construction is confusing, and its use is not recommended.

4. If there is a file called *module-name*.so Pike will load that file with load_module(), clone it, and use the newly-cloned object as a module. The file should be a dynamically linkable library of compiled C or C++ code.

As we said before, you usually don't need to worry about these details, except for what is needed to put your modules somewhere where Pike can find them.

Exercises

1. Write a program that reads a file using the Stdio module, and then prints the file line by line with the line number prepended to each line.

2. Write a program that uses datatypes from the Protocols.HTTP module to load a URL and print the server's response code.

3. Create a new module that contains functions for squaring two integers, and removing double spaces from strings.

4. Experiment with the various ways that you can alter the locations that Pike looks for modules. Test these methods by moving your module from the previous exercies to different directories.

5. What happens if there are two modules in your module path with the same name? Can you access both?

Errors and Error Handling

When you complete this chapter, you should be able to:

1. Explain two ways that Pike can pass information about the occurrence of an error to other parts of a program.

2. Write code that traps errors thrown by code you use, as well as send your own errors to other parts of a program.

No matter how carefully planned and written your code is, you will eventually encounter an error. Luckily, Pike provides facilities for dealing with errors, as well as producing your own.

Errors Messages from Pike

When Pike encounters an error that it can't handle, or finds something suspicious in a program, you may get a **warning** or an **error message**. A warning is a piece of text that Pike prints in order to inform you of a potential problem. An error message is printed when a problem occurs that prevents the program from continuing.

Your program can also print its own warnings and error messages, but first we look at messages that Pike itself prints when it reads and examines your program.

Most warnings are about possible problems with data types. For example, let us assume the following three variable definitions:

```
mixed m;
```

Pike: an Introduction

```
string s;
int i;
```

In that case, the following assignment will give a warning:

```
i = m;
```

The variable m can contain any type of value, but i can only contain integer values, so Pike warns you that there is a possible problem. For example, what would happen if m contains a string?

Warning messages follow the pattern

```
filename:line-number: Warning: description
```

so the warning message that is printed will look something like this:

```
ex3.pike:17: Warning: An expression type mixed
cannot be assigned to a variable of type int.
```

Warnings and error messages are not printed on the standard output, but on the standard error output. Even if you re-direct the output from a program, the standard error output is usually printed on the screen.

Given the same three variable definitions, this expression gives an error and not just a warning:

```
i = s;
```

The error message looks something like this:

```
ex3.pike:21:Bad type in assignment.
ex3.pike:21:Expected: int
```

```
ex3.pike:21:Got       : string
Pike: Failed to compile script:
Compilation failed.
```

Error messages are always printed, and will cause the program to terminate. By default, warnings are *not* printed. They are turned off by default, and you have to turn them on.

To turn on warnings for the code in a certain file, you can add the line

```
#pragma strict_types
```

to that file. An alternative is to give the command-line argument -rT to Pike, which turns on warnings for all files, even those that are used from your program. An example:

```
pike -rT myprogram.pike
```

This will print all warnings that Pike is able to generate for the file myprogram.pike, and for all other files (such as modules) that it uses.

It is usually a very good idea to turn on warnings, at least during program development. Why would you *not* let the computer help you find the bugs in your program?

Pike: an Introduction

Your own error messages

When you examine a program that is intended to solve a real problem in the real world, a surprisingly large portion of the program will be written just to take care of possible errors. Even in the simple web browser from the example earlier in this introduction, which hardly qualifies as a real-world program, we had to handle no less than three possible errors:

- An incorrect number of command-line arguments to the program.

- The user didn't write a web address, and just pressed the return key instead.

- The browser couldn't download the web page from the given address.

Error handling usually consists of two parts: **detecting** the error, and **handling** it.

Detecting an Error

In the web browser, we detected the first two possible errors by checking the data: the number of command-line arguments, and the length of the web address that the user types.

In the third case, when a web page couldn't be downloaded, the problem is detected somewhere inside the function `get_url()` in the module `Protocols.HTTP`. The problem must then be reported to the program that called `get_url()`, and this is done with the **return value**. The function `get_url()` usually returns an object with the data from the web page, but if it fails to retrieve the web page, it returns zero (**0**):

```
web_page = Protocols.HTTP.get_url(this_url);
if(web_page == 0)
{
 write(" Failed.\n");
 return;
}
```

The value **zero** is just the normal integer 0, but it is used in many contexts to mean "no value" or "there was a problem". Many of the built-in functions in Pike return 0 if they fail to do what they are supposed to do. Most Pike programmers use the same convention.

To work this way, the integer 0 has to be special. It can be stored in a variable of any type, and it can be returned from any function. Every new variable that you define will contain the value 0, until you give it another value.

Handling the Error

After an error is detected, it can be handled in different ways. The web browser uses two ways: trying again, and terminating the program with an error message. If the user gave a zero-length web address, the program asks again.

If you want to terminate the program, this is a common code snippet:

```
if(result_of_something == 0)
{
```

Pike: an Introduction

```
werror("Failed to open the file '" + file_name + "'\n");
exit(1);
}
```

Calling exit() will terminate the program. Returning a value greater than 0 from main() or as an argument to exit() means that the program failed in some way.

The built-in function werror() prints a string on the **standard error output** (Stdio.stderr) instead of the normal **standard output** (Stdio.stdout). This has a higher chance of being seen by the user, since if you re-direct the output from a program, like this:

```
webbrowser.pike cod.ida.liu.se > output.txt
```

then the standard output will be printed to the file output.txt, but the standard error output will still be printed on the screen.

Error Codes

The return value 0 from a function may show that there was some error, but not what the problem was. It is common to combine return values of this kind with a way to find out the nature of the problem. This can be done with special **error codes**, that your program can retrieve from somewhere. Let's look at this example, which opens a file on disk for reading:

```
Stdio.File localfile = Stdio.File();
if(!localfile->open(file_name, "r"))
{
```

```
werror("Couldn't open '" + file_name + "'.\n");
  werror(strerror(localfile->errno()) +
         " (errno = " + localfile->errno() + ").\n");
  exit(1);
 }
```

Some comments about this code:

- `Stdio.File` is a stream that can be used to read from a file on fisk. It is similar to the data type `FILE` in C, and the classes `ifstream` and `ofstream` in C++.

- `!localfile->open(file_name, "r")` means exactly the same thing as `localfile->open(file_name, "r") == 0`.

- It is common to use the **logical not** operator (`!`) to check if something is 0.

- `errno()` is a function in the class `Stdio.File`, and can be used to check what kind of error has occurred in a particular stream. It returns an error code. `errno()` is not a global variable, as in C.

- `strerror()` returns a string that describes the error number given as an argument.

If the file couldn't be opened, the program's output will look something like this:

```
Couldn't open 'foobar.txt'.
```

Pike: an Introduction

```
No such file or directory (errno = 2).
```

Exceptions with Catch and Throw

It is not uncommon that we want to separate the detection and the handling of errors. The place where an error can be detected is not always the place where it is best handled. Take for example the function `Protocols.HTTP.get_url()`. It is easy for that function to detect when a web page couldn't be retrieved, but how should that problem be handled? This depends on the program that wanted the web page, so `get_url()`, which is in a module that will be used by many programs, can't know what to do. Instead, it returns the value 0, in order to inform the calling program that it failed, and thereby it leaves the responsibility for handling the problem to the calling program.

Many functions work this way: you have to check the returned value to see if the function succeeded or not. If you don't let your program check every return value from every function call, an error may be detected and reported by one of those functions, but never handled. Depending on what type of error it was, all kinds of unpleasant things can happen.

An improvement over this "return-value checking" style of error handling is **exceptions**. When a problem is detected, perhaps inside a function somewhere deep inside a module, the code can **throw an exception**:

```
if(result_of_something == 0)
  throw("Failed to open the file called '" +
        file_name + "'\n");
```

If this is all that is done, the program will be terminated. But the nice thing is that you may not only **throw** an exception, you may **catch** it too! This is done by enclosing the code that called the exception-throwing function in a **catch block**:

```
mixed result = catch {
    i = klooble() + 2;
    fnooble();
    j = 1/i;
};
if(result == 0)
    write("Everything was ok.\n");
else
    write("Oops. There was an error.\n");
```

Note that the catch block is an **expression**, unlike ordinary blocks which are **statements**, so we have to use a semi-colon to end the **expression statement**.

If no exceptions are thrown during the execution of the catch block, it just executes to the end like any normal block. The block returns a value, which in our example will be put in the variable result. If no exceptions are thrown, the return value from the catch block is 0.

If an exception *was* thrown, either in the catch block itself, or in one of the functions called from the catch block, or in one of the functions called from those functions, and so on, then execution of the catch block will terminate, and the return value of the catch block will be the argument that was given to throw(), in our case the string "Failed to open the file called 'some file-name'\n".

Pike: an Introduction

A good thing with exceptions is that they can be thrown "through" a function. Even if that function doesn't do any error checking at all, the exception will be propagated to the caller. An an example, study this partial program:

```
void drink_coffee()
{
   if(coffe_pot == 0)
     throw("No coffe-pot.");
}


void eat_dinner()
{
   eat_main_course();
   eat_dessert();
   drink_coffee();
}
int main()
{
   mixed result = catch
   {
     eat_dinner();
   };
   if(result == 0)
     write("Everything was ok.\n");
   else
     write("There was an error: " + result + "\n");
   return 0;
```

```
}
```

The function main() calls eat_dinner(), which in turn calls drink_coffee(). If drink_coffee() discovers that the coffee-pot is missing, it will throw an exception. This exception will pass right through eat_dinner(), and be caught in main().

If we hadn't used exceptions, but return codes instead, and if we assume that things can go wrong in all the functions, then eat_dinner() would have looked something like this:

```
int eat_dinner()
{
  if(!eat_main_course())
    return 0;
  if(!eat_dessert())
    return 0;
  if(!drink_coffee())
    return 0;
  return 1;
}
```

As we can see, the version with exceptions is much simpler and easier, both to write and to understand.

It is a good practice to always examine the return value of a catch. Because catch does not allow you to specify which type of error you want to catch, you may inadvertently hide an error that you did not intend to handle.

Pike: an Introduction

Built-in exceptions and error objects

The Pike interpreter can throw its own exceptions. For example, an attempt to divide by zero will throw an exception. Most of these "internal" exceptions are objects, with a number of functions and member variables that you can use to determine the nature of the problem that caused the exception. These error objects are defined in the `Error` module.

If the caught exception is an object, you can use the member variable `error_type` to get the name of the type of this error, for example "math_error". You can also use the function `describe()` in the exception object, to get a string with a short descriptive text, that presents the error in a way suitable for presenting to a human: the error message, and the chain of functions that were called. Look at this excerpt from a function for an example:

```
mixed result = catch
{
  koogle(0, 3.0, "foo");
};
if(result == 0)
  write("Everything was ok.\n");
else if(objectp(result))
{
  write("There was an error.\n");
  write("Type of error: " + result->error_type + "\n");
  write("Description of the error:\n");
  write(result->describe());
  write("Done.\n");
```

```
}
else
{
  write("There was some other type of error.\n");
}
```

Even more interesting, though, is that you can define your own exception objects. By making a subclass of `Error.Generic`, or by creating your own error object from the scratch, you can pass information about your errors to the functions that `catch()` them. Especially useful is the ability to provide identifiers in your custom error objects to allow you to differentiate various types of errors. You can also use `object_program()` to determine the type of error object thrown. The following example code demonstrates ways of determining the type of error object you've been thrown.

```
int some_function()
{
    mixed e = catch(function_that_throws_errors());
    if(e && object_program(e) == Error.Math)
      werror("we caught a math error!\n" + e->description());

    // we could do it by looking for an identifier, too
    else if(e && e->is_custom_error)
      werror("we caught a custom error!\n" + e->description());
}
```

Pike: an Introduction

In order to throw a custom error object, you just need to pass an object to the
`throw()` function:

```
int function_that_throws_errors()
{
  if(random(10) > 5)
     throw(Error.Generic("We randomly throw errors.\n"));
}
```

Exercises

1. Explain the difference between a warning and an error. Write code that
    generates each.

2. Write a function that returns a true boolean value on success and a false
    value on failure. Write a program that calls this function and reports ac-
    cordingly based on that return value.

3. Write a program that throws errors.

4. Modify the program from the previous exercise so that the errors are
    caught and handled by writing a friendly message to the screen.

5. Create a program that contains a custom error type that inherits `Error.-`
    `Generic`. Throw errors of your custom error type to the calling function,
    which should catch the error and detect the error type.

Commonly Used Modules

When you finish this chapter, you should be able to:

1. Create a database connection and run queries.

2. Create an image object from an image file.

3. Read data from a file on disk and then write it back to disk.

This chapter won't cover all of the modules included with Pike, but it will arm you with some useful tools that you can use in your own programs, and will give you a head start into using the large collection of modules available with Pike. This chapter will cover some common operations that you'll probably encounter a need for while developing your own Pike applications.

Please note that we will not be covering every technique or way of using a module or function, only the most commonly used ones. Many of these modules have a great deal of flexibility, and we'd be able to fill this book many times over if we did. Once you're up and running with a module, be sure to check out the Pike module reference, available online at the Pike website.

Database Access

Pike has built in support for a variety of SQL database systems, depending on how your Pike was configured. This support is found in the SQL module and makes it simple to work with relational databases. The benefit of Pike's database access support is that all databases use the same API. This means that if you write database independent SQL, you can switch databases at will without changing your code.

SQL URLs

In order to connect to a database, Pike needs to know what type of database to connect to, as well as any credentials such as username or database name. This information is encoded in a SQL URL. SQL URLs are constructed in the following way:

```
dbtype://username:password@host/dbname
```

Technically speaking, only *dbtype* and *host* are required however, most databases will need one or more of the others as well. Exactly how or whether you'll use these fields will depend on the type of database you're connecting to. For example, an Oracle database URL might look like this:

```
oracle://scott:tiger@globalidentifier
```

while a mysql database URL might be:

```
mysql://root@localhost/test
```

Connecting to a database

Once you've prepared a SQL URL for the database you want to access, you'll need to make a connection to it. All database access is performed using the `Sql.Sql` class. To make a connection, pass the URL as an argument to the class's constructor:

```
Sql.Sql dbconn = Sql.Sql("oracle://scott:tiger@prod01");
```

If an error occurs while connecting, an exception will be thrown. If all goes well, you should have a live database connection.

Querying a database

Once you have a `Sql.Sql` object, chances are you'll want to perform some queries. Pike has two functions for querying a database, depending on the needs of your application and the amount of data that your queries will return. The first function is a simple query that returns any results in an array of mappings. The other function, called `big_query()`, returns an object that can be used to retrieve the results. `big_query()` only retrieves data from the result set when you request it, assuming it's supported by your database. This is useful when your result sets might be extermely large as Pike won't have to allocate memory for the entire result set at once. We'll cover the easier one first, and then give some basics for using `big_query()`. Here's an example to get a list of all your bookmarks from the Pike homepage:

```
string query="select Shortcut, URL from bookmarks where "
    " Hostname='pike.ida.liu.se'";
array result = dbconn->query(q);
```

In this example code, result will contain 1 array element for each row of data returned. If the query returned no data, result will be set to 0. You can use loops such as `foreach` to loop through each row in the result set. Each row is represented as a mapping, with an index for each field returned by the database. Pike will return the values from the database as a string, regardless of what type the data is in the database. You can use value casting to manipulate the types of data. A hypothetical result set might look like this:

Pike: an Introduction

```
({

  (["Shortcut": "reference", "URL":
"http://pike.ida.liu.se/generated/manual/modref/"]),

  (["Shortcut": "pikefarm", "URL":
"http://pike.ida.liu.se/development/pikefarm/7.6.xml"])

})
```

Now that you have a set of results, you'll probably want to do something with them. As an example, you could write a `foreach` loop that writes the result to your screen:

```
foreach(result; ; mapping row)

  write("bookmark: " + row->Shortcut + " " +

    row->URL + "\n");
```

As you can see, using a simple query gives you a very simple way of working with query results. The drawback is that Pike has to process the entire result set and create mappings for each row before you get the result back. For large results, this can create a significant amount of delay.

Using big_query()

When you're planning on running queries that return large amounts of data, particularly if the amount of data would cause the Pike interpreter to run out of memory, using a simple query isn't a viable option. Luckily, the clever programmers who developed Pike's database access layer came up with a way around the problem.

The solution involves the use of `big_query()`, which returns its results as a `sql_result` object. The object has functions that allow you to navigate the result set, which allows Pike to transfer data from the database as you request it, rather than all at once. This saves memory and processing time, because Pike doesn't have to transfer all of the data and prepare the result mappings before you get the results. The downside is that the query result object takes a little bit more work to use.

Getting a result object is simple. We can modify our earlier example to return a `sql_result` object:

```
string query="select Shortcut, URL from bookmarks where "
  " Hostname='pike.ida.liu.se'";
Sql.sql_result result = dbconn->big_query(q);
```

Now you may use the `sql_result` object to navigate and retrieve rows from the result set. The most important functions are: `num_rows()`, `fetch_row()`, and `seek()`. `num_rows()` will return an integer telling you the number of rows in the result. If the query doesn't return any rows (like an INSERT query, or if no matching rows were found) it will return 0. `fetch_row()` will return a mapping containing the fields in the next row of result data. The mapping is similar to the mapping returned for each row by `query()`. Finally, `seek()` will skip a given number of rows in the result set. We'll modify the previous loop example to work with a `sql_result` object:

```
for(int i=0; i<result->num_rows(); i++)
{
  mapping row = result->fetch_row();
  write("bookmark: " + row->Shortcut + " " +
    row->URL + "\n");
}
```

Pike: an Introduction

As you can see, it's not terribly difficult to use a `sql_result` object, and it gives you complete control over what part of the result set you want to process and when. If your database does not support delayed retrieval of rows from the result set, you may still use `big_query()`, only you will not be able to benefit from the lower memory usage.

Quoting

Sooner or later, you will run into data for a query that contains characters that are considered special by your database. Examples of this include quotation marks and newlines. There are 2 ways to ensure that your data will be properly escaped. The first involves manually quoting the data using the `quote()` function. The second is an automatic function that also makes it easier to write queries.

Using the `quote()` function is pretty simple. In the following example, `bad_value` contains a character (the apostrophe) that will cause a SQL error if not properly escaped:

```
string bad_value="O'Brian";

array result = dbconn->query("SELECT * FROM mytable WHERE
Last_Name = '" + dbconn->quote(bad_value) + "'");
```

This method, while effective, requires you to manually run the `quote()` function on any data that might have charaters requiring escaping. Obviously, that's not a very efficient way of handling the problem.

The second method involves using format strings to parameterize the query. This technique is similar to using `sprintf()`, and makes writing queries simple. Here's an example:

```
string bad_value="O'Brian";
array result = dbconn->query("SELECT * FROM mytable WHERE "
  "Last_Name = %s and Age = %d", bad_value, 44);
```

If you provide more than one argument to query(), the first argument will be searched for format identifiers, such as %s for a string or %d for an integer, and the corresponding value will be quoted and inserted in the resulting query. Note that you don't have to put quotation marks around strings, the query builder knows how your database engine expects values of a certain type to be presented. Also, you must provide the values as the correct data types. That is, if you specify %d, the corresponding parameter must be an integer.

Pike Cryptography

Pike contains a complete cryptographic toolkit, with support for a wide variety of hash and cipher algorithms. All of the crypto types use a common api, so you can interchange algorithms (within reason) without having to change large amounts of code.

Hashes

Pike has support for a large number of commonly used hash algorithms, such as MD5 and SHA1, among others. Hashes allow you to take a large amount of data and reduce (or digest) it into a much shorter string.

Ideally, you should not be able to recreate the original string from that digested string. Additionally, there should be relatively few collisions, that is, few situations

Pike: an Introduction

where two strings result in the same digest. Hashes are frequently used to check passwords, as well as to verify authenticity of a given set of data.

The process of creating or verifying a hash begins with the creation of a hash object. This is relatively simple, you just pick an algorithm, say SHA1, and create the corresponding object:

```
object h = Crypto.SHA1();
```

This gives you an initialized hash object that is ready to accept some data to digest. To add data to a hash, you simply send it some data using update():

```
h->update("Some data to hash");
```

This adds the given string to the hash. You can call update() as many times as you wish before generating the final hash. All data fed to the hash object will be used to generate the final digested value. To generate the digest, simply call digest():

```
string digest = h->digest();
```

Calling digest will generate a digest using the chosen algorithm, and will then reset the hash's contents for reuse. The result is a binary string, which may be used directly, or (as is often the case,) encoded for easy transmission to another party. You can also pass an integer to digest(), which will cause the digest to be truncated to that number of bytes. Normally, though, you wouldn't do that and would work with the full value produced.

For each of the hash algorithms, sending the same set of data to a hash object in its "starting" state will produce the same digested string. This means that you can verify that a given set of data has not been tampered with by taking the data and running it through a hash algorithm. If the value from the first hash is the same as the second, you know that the data has not been altered. For example:

```
// what we expect to get string
string original = "the original text";


// someone has tampered with the data
string modified = "the Original text";


string h = Crypto.SHA1()->update(original)->digest();
string h1 = Crypto.SHA1()->update(modified)->digest();
if(h!=h1)
  write("The data has been tampered with!\n");
else
  write("The data has arrived intact!\n");
```

In this example, the original data and the second set of data are not identical, which means that their hashes will be different. Notice that we've "pipelined" several functions together. This is possible because the functions within hash objects have been specially designed to return the hash object itself. This makes it possible to tie several functions together, as update() returns the hash object we're working with, so that we can call digest() from that updated object. This design feature makes it easy to bundle a set of function calls into one statement.

Encrypting and Decrypting

The Crypto module contains a large number of symmetric ciphers, such as AES (Rijndael) and ARCFour. These ciphers allow you to encrypt and decrypt data using the same key. These algorithms are commonly used to encrypt traffic between two hosts after the key has been negotiated with a public key algorithm such as RSA. All of the symmetric ciphers share a common API, so just as you can swap hash algorithms, you can (within reason) do the same with ciphers.

The first step in encrypting data is to create a cipher object. Select the algorithm you want to use, and create the object:

```
object c = Crypto.AES();
```

There are a number of useful functions within the cipher object. make_key() prepares a key by generating a random string, and then initializes the cipher for encryption using that key. The key that is generated is returned by make_key(). Note that each algorithm has different rules for key length, so this function will return a different key length depending on the cipher in use.

set_encrypt_key() and set_decrypt_key() are used to initialize the cipher object for encryption and decryption, respectively. They take as arguments a key in the correct format for the chosen cipher.

crypt() is used to encrypt or decrypt the data passed as an argument, depending on whether the cipher object is set to encrypt or decrypt. Note that if you are using a block cipher, you must send data to crypt() in increments of the block size for the cipher.

key_size() returns the size of the key in use as a string.

Note that the cipher objects also provide two shortcuts: encrypt() and decrypt(). The first argument for each function is the key, and the second argument should be the data to encrypt or decrypt, respectively. These allow you to quickly perform an operation without having to manually initialize the cipher object's behavior. For example:

```
object cipher = Cipher.ArcFour();
string key = make_key();
string beginning = "starting out...";
write("original data: " + beginning + "\n");
string enc = cipher->encrypt(key, beginning);
write("encrypted data: " + enc + "\n");
// we should end up with what we started with.
string dec = cipher->decrypt(key, enc);
write("decrypted data: " + dec + "\n");
```

As you can see, the cryptography support included with Pike is powerful, yet easy to use because of a common API for all ciphers and hashes. This allows you to choose the best algorithm for the task without having to learn intricate details of each one.

Pike also includes functions for performing buffering when using block ciphers (Crypto.Buffer), as well as popular public key algorithms (such as Crypto.R-SA). We won't cover these topics here, but we've armed you with the information you need to productively use large parts of the Crypto module.

Working with Processes

The Process module provides functions and classes for working with external processes. Situations where you might need to use this module might include run-

Pike: an Introduction

ning a command and placing the output into a string, or starting a program and waiting until it completes. We'll cover two functions and one class that you'll use most often when working with external processes: `Process.system()`, `Process.popen()` and `Process.create_process`.

When you want to run a program in a shell and receive the return code as a return value, you should use `Process.system()`. This function is the analogue of the similarly named system call provided by most operating systems. The function is used as follows:

```
int retval = Process.system("touch /tmp/test.txt");
```

In this example, we're running a command line program and providing it with an argument, just as though you'd typed it into your command shell. In fact, the `system()` function starts a shell that your command is then run in. The function returns an integer that represents the return code from the program.

Sometimes, you need to get the output of the command and use it within your program. To fill this need, Pike provides the `Process.popen()` function. This function is similar to the `Process.system()` function discussed previously, except its return value is a string that contains the standard output of the command. You can use it like this:

```
string output = Process.popen("ls -l /etc");
write("output: " + output + "\n");
```

In this example, we run the `ls` command to get a detailed directory listing of the `/etc` directory. The function runs the command and returns the output of the command as a string.

The create_process class

In addition to simple process execution functions, Pike also provides a more advanced process manipulation class. This class, `Process.create_process`, gives you more complete control over the execution of an external process. You can specify CPU and clock time limits on the process, redirect its input and output streams to Pike file objects, and other advanced modifications to a process' lifecycle. The class is used in the following manner:

```
Process.create_process( array command, mapping modifiers );
```

Where *command* is an array containing the program name, plus any arguments for the program. The mapping *modifiers* is used to pass additional parameters that specify how the process is run. For example:

```
mapping modifiers = (["cwd" : "/tmp", "nice" : 10]);
object process = Process.create_process(
({"/usr/bin/edit","test.txt"}),

    modifiers );
```

The process object created will be immediately returned, and provides a number of functions that you can use to examine and control the process, the most important of which are `kill()`, `pid()`, `status()` and `wait()`.

`kill()` is used to send a signal to the running process. It takes an integer as an argument. The argument represents the signal number you want to send to the process. You can use the `signum()` function to convert a symbolic (text) signal name to the signal number. For example:

```
process->kill(signum("SIGKILL"));
```

Pike: an Introduction

Will send the KILL signal to the running process. You can get the process id (PID) of the process by calling the function pid(). This function will return the PID as an integer. For example:

```
write("the process id is : " + process->pid() + "\n");
```

You can check on the status of a running program using the status() function. This function will return an integer describing the current state of the process: 0 if the process is running, 2 if the process exited normally, or 1 if the process was terminated. If Pike has somehow lost track of the process, status() will return -1. Normally, though, this shouldn't happen.

Finally, you can use the wait() function to wait for the process to exit. If the process has already exited, wait() will return immediately. The return value of wait() is the return value of the process, or -1 if the process was killed. For example:

```
if(process->wait()>=0)
  write("the process ended normally\n");
else
  write("the process was killed.\n");
```

As you can see, Pike gives you a wide range of process control options, ranging from the quick and easy, to more advanced tools that give you complete control over the life cycle of a process. You can learn more about these tools and others by viewing the Process module documentation contained in the Pike module reference.

Interacting with files using Stdio

Stdio is probably the most commonly used module. It provides functions and classes for performing all manner of I/O, including file and network based data transfer. We'll only begin to scratch the surface of this valuable module, as this could be the subject of a book by itself. We'll discuss techniques for reading and writing files, as well as for looking at the metadata for a file.

Atomic file operations

For quick and easy access to a file there are three convenience functions located within the Stdio module: Stdio.read_file(), Stdio.write_file(), and Stdio.append_file(). Each one of these performs an "atomic" operation, that is, reading a file into a string, writing a string to a file, or appending a string to a file. You only need to use one statement to perform the action. For example:

```
string data=Stdio.read_file("/tmp/data.txt");
```

will open the file "/tmp/data.txt" read its contents and assign them to the string data. When the function is done, the file will be closed.

The following statement:

```
Stdio.write_file("/tmp/data.txt", data);
```

will do just the opposite, that is, write the contents of the string data to the file "/tmp/data.txt". The file will be created if it didn't already exist, and the file's contents will be completely replaced with data.

Pike: an Introduction

As you might guess, `Stdio.append_file()` will append a string to the end of a file. It's used in the following way:

```
Stdio.append_file("/tmp/data.txt", data);
```

Working with file objects

In addition to the simple functions described above, Pike provides an object oriented interface to files. The two classes that can be used to manipulate files are called `Stdio.File` for non-buffered access and `Stdio.FILE` for buffered file access. Both classes have a similar API, with minor adjustments for the buffered nature of `Stdio.FILE`. We'll only be covering non-buffered access here, but you'll be able to pick up the differences pretty readily.

The first step in working with any file in Pike is to create a file object. In order to do this, pass the filename you'd like to open, along with the access mode you want to use, to the constructor of the class. For example,

```
Stdio.File data=Stdio.File("/tmp/data.txt", "rw");
```

will open the file "/tmp/data.txt" for reading and writing. If a problem occurred while opening the file, such as a permission problem, an exception will be thrown. For example, if we try to open a file that we don't have permission to view, we get the following:

```
$ pike
Pike v7.6 release 13 running Hilfe v3.5 (Incremental Pike
Frontend)
> object S=Stdio.File("/etc/shadow", "r");
Failed to open "/etc/shadow" mode "r" : Permission denied
/usr/local/pike/7.6.13/lib/modules/Stdio.pmod/module.pmod:6
```

```
52: Stdio.File("/etc/shadow", 0, 777 /* fd=-1 */)-
>create("/etc/shadow","r",438)
/usr/local/pike/7.6.13/lib/modules/Stdio.pmod/module.pmod:1
805: Stdio->File()
```

However, if all went well, you should have a new Stdio.File object. You may now begin reading from the file:

```
string somedata=data->read(10);
```

will read the first 10 bytes from data. To write data, you can use the write() function:

```
data->write("overwriting");
```

will start writing from the point where you last stopped reading. There's always a possibility of a problem occurring during a read or write, so you should be prepared to check the returned values from each function, or catch any exceptions that might be thrown. If you want to move to a particular part of the file, you can use the seek() function, which will move to a given position of the file:

```
file->seek(24);
```

will move to the 25th byte of the file (if it exists). Remember that Pike starts counting at zero, so if you want to move to the beginning of the file, you should seek() to position **0**.

Often you will want to read a file line by line. An iterator combined with foreach makes this task efficient and easy:

```
foreach(datafile->line_iterator();; string line)
  write(reverse(line)+"\n");
```

Pike: an Introduction

`Stdio` also provides interfaces to **standard input**, **standard output**, and **standard error output**. The default `write()` is actually a shortcut for `Stdio.stdout->write()`. Here is an example for a pipe:

```
#!/usr/local/bin/pike
void main()
{
  string input;
  int count;
  while(input=Stdio.stdin->gets())
  {
    write(reverse(input)+"\n");
    count++;
  }
  werror("reversed %d lines\n", count);
}
```

This will read lines from standard input, reverse them, and write them back to standard output. Save this in a file called "reverse.pike" and use it like this:

```
$ chmod a+rx reverse.pike
$ cat data.txt | reverse.pike > reversed_data.txt
reversed 20 lines
$
```

When you're finished working with a file (reading or writing,) you should always close the file. To do this, we use the `close()` function:

```
file->close();
```

Once you close a file, you can't do anything with it until you open it again, either by creating a new `Stdio.File` object, or by using the `open()` function contained within an existing `Stdio.File` object. We won't provide an example of `open()`, but it takes the same arguments as the constructor of the `Stdio.File` class.

Viewing file metadata

You can query a file or directory's metadata by using the `file_stat()` function. This function will look up a file and, if it exists, return a `Stdio.Stat` object that contains information about the path. You can access ownership information, as well as modification dates and permissions:

```
Stdio.Stat s = Stdio.file_stat("/etc/passwd");
if(!s)
  write("file doesn't exist\n");
else
  write("size: " + s->size + "\nmodified: "
    + s->mtime + "\n");
```

You can view the complete list of elements in this object by referring to the Pike module reference.

Communicating with network sockets

Pike also provides powerful tools for performing communication over a network. You can very easily connect to a host using TCP/IP and communicate back and forth using `Stdio.File` objects. The technique for doing this is only slightly different than working with files on disk. To start the process, we need a new

Pike: an Introduction

`Stdio.File` object. However, we don't want to actually open a file, so we leave the constructor empty:

```
Stdio.File my_socket = Stdio.File();
```

Now, once we have a file object ready to go, we can connect using the appropriately named `connect()` function. For example, to connect to the webserver at www.gotpike.org (which is running on port 80 of that host), we'd write the following:

```
int result = my_socket->connect("www.gotpike.org", 80);
```

The `connect()` function will attempt to open a TCP connection to port 80 of the host "www.gotpike.org". If the connect was successful, `connect()` will return 1, otherwise, it will return 0. You can then use `errno()` to find the resulting error code.

When you have an open connection to a remote port, you can read and write data back and forth, just as you would work with a file. Do note that you can't use `seek()` on a network stream. Also, you should know that if you try to read more data than the other host has written, `read()` will wait, or "**block**" until enough data is available. To get around this problem, you can pass a second argument to the `read()` function:

```
my_socket->read(25, 1);
```

passing 1 as the second argument to `read()` will tell Pike to only read as many bytes as is available. That means you could get 25 bytes if there were at least 25 bytes ready when you called `read()`, or you'll get whatever was in the read buffer at the time. Unless you know exactly how the other end will respond, you should never issue a read with no arguments, as you could be left waiting until the other host closes the connection.

As we did when we were finished working with a file, we should always call close() to close the connection with the remote host:

```
my_socket->close();
```

Using the HTTP protocol module

One of the first Pike programs we presented was a simple web browser application. The core functionality of the application (speaking the HTTP protocol to a remote server) was provided courtesy of the Protocols.HTTP module. This module has a large number of useful classes and functions, including a simple web server class (which we won't cover here). We'll discuss some of the functions from the module, as well as from the related XML-RPC module.

Performing GET and POST queries

By far the most common HTTP requests are the GET and POST methods. Pike provides a set of functions for performing both of these requests. Additionally, as with the SQL module, there are simple query functions and lower level query functions that provide an object interface.

There are two variations of the simple get and post functions provided by Protocols.HTTP. One returns a string containing the data returned by the server; these are get_url_data() and post_url_data(), and the other returns an array containing the mime type of the data as well as the data itself; these are

Pike: an Introduction

`get_url_nice()` and `post_url_nice()`. If redirects are sent by the server, they will be followed. All of these functions take the same set of arguments, which we will describe using `get_url_data()` as an example.

```
string Protocols.HTTP.get_url_nice(string|Standards.URI url,
    mapping(string:int|string) query_variables,
    mapping(string:string|array(string)) request_headers,
    void|Protocols.HTTP.Query con))
```

`url` is either a string containing the URL you wish to act on, or a `Standards.URI` object. We haven't covered this class, so we won't use it here.

`query_variables` is an optional mapping containing variable name and variable value pairs you wish to submit to the server. If you are using a GET function, these will be appended to the URL in the appropriate fashion. If you're using a POST function, the query variables will be encoded and passed to the server as part of the request data.

`request_headers` is an optional mapping containing header name to header value pairs. If the header value is an array, the header will be repeated so that each value is sent in its own header line.

`con` is an optional `Protocols.HTTP.Query` object that can be provided to the request function. If the `Query` object is part of a keep-alive request, the request function will reuse the connection provided by the `Query` object in order to cut down on network traffic.

Here is a simple example of a GET request:

```
string result = Protocols.HTTP.get_url_data(
```

```
"http://modules.gotpike.org/modules.html",
(["module_id": 21]));
```

In this example, we're retrieving a URL and passing a query variable using a GET request. The contents of the "file" we've requested will be returned as a string. The functions `get_url_nice()` and `post_url_nice()` work similarly, with the exception that the returned value is an array. The first element in the array is the MIME type of the data, which is the second element in the returned array.

As we mentioned earlier, Pike also provides an interface to HTTP requests that is more low-level. These functions, `get_url()` and `post_url()` return a Protocols.HTTP.Query object that you can use to view the result of the query. When using these functions, you will receive the result for the URL requested and will see the return codes, so if a redirect is sent, it will not be followed and will be reflected in the returned Query object.

The low level functions take the same arguments as the high level request functions, so we won't repeat their description. We will only discuss the Query object here, as we've covered the other relevant pieces in the previous section.

Here's an example using the Query interface:

```
Protocols.HTTP.Query q = Protocols.HTTP.get_url(
    "http://www.gotpike.org");
```

If we run this command in hilfe (interactive pike), we can see the object returned:

```
> Protocols.HTTP.Query q = Protocols.HTTP.get_url
("http://www.gotpike.org");
> q;
```

Pike: an Introduction

```
(1) Result: Protocols.HTTP.Query(302 Temporary Relocation)
```

As you can see, our request resulted in a temporary relocation response (in other words, we got a redirect).

There are a number of useful members in the Query object:

headers is a mapping of all of the headers sent by the server in response to the request. All of the header names are in lower case for ease of use. In our example query, we know that the "Location" header contains the destination that we're being redirected to, so we can see where the file has been moved to:

```
> q->headers["location"];
(8) Result: "http://www.gotpike.org/index.html"
```

In this case, we can see where the redirect is pointing, so we can issue another GET request with this new location if we wanted to get the file.

errno is an integer containing the HTTP result code. In the case of our request above, this will contain **302**.

data() will return the data returned by the server. If our query had resulted in a "200 OK" response (that is, the file was found), calling data() would give us the file we requested.

Casting the Query object to a string will result in the full response from the server:

```
> (string)q;
```

```
(7) Result: "HTTP/1.0 302 Temporary Relocation\r\nServer:
Caudium/1.5.1  DEVEL\r\nLocation:
http://www.gotpike.org/(SessionID=0c6cb5345da13bd12a4218c43
c0dccb8)/\r\nDate: Thu, 30 Sep 2004 22:10:23
GMT\r\nContent-Length: 0\r\nX-Got-Fish: Pike v7.6 release
13\r\nConnection: close\r\nContent-Type:
text/html\r\nAccept-Ranges: bytes\r\nMIME-Version:
1.0\r\nSet-Cookie:
SessionID=0c6cb5345da13bd12a4218c43c0dccb8; path=/;
Expires=Fri, 31 Dec 2010 23:59:59 GMT;\r\n\r\n"
```

The `Query` object has many other members that can be called into service at the appropriate time, but these will get you started. For more details, check out the Pike module reference.

XML-RPC support

Pike provides a module that provides support for XML-RPC (remote procedure call). XML-RPC allows non-similar systems to call procedures remotely across the internet. The specification uses HTTP and XML as transport and encoding, respectively. There are clients and servers for many operating systems and languages. Pike provides support for XML-RPC clients and servers, though we'll only be discussing the client here.

The client is available in the class `Protocols.XMLRPC.Client`. To create a new XMLRPC client, simply pass the URL of the service provider to the class constructor. Here's an example that uses a public time provider:

```
object x=Protocols.XMLRPC.Client(

  "http://time.xmlrpc.com/RPC2");
```

Pike: an Introduction

Once you have a client object, you can call functions provided by the XML-RPC provider you selected when creating the object. To call a remote function, you use the following construct:

```
array returnvalue = client[methodname](args);
```

where methodname is the XML-RPC method you wish to call, and args are the arguments to the method. Our example uses a function called "current-Time.getCurrentTime", and takes no arguments. Any return value will be returned to you in the array returnvalue. For example:

```
> x["currentTime.getCurrentTime"]();
(2) Result: ({ /* 1 element */
               Second(Thu 30 Sep 2004 17:34:48 EDT)
           })
```

As you can see, this XML-RPC function call returns a Calendar object for the current time, which is wrapped in an array. Pike performs a number of type translations to and from Pike and XML-RPC datatypes. For details of these conversions, refer to the Pike module reference.

The Image module

Pike has extensive support for working with images. This support is found in the Image module, and includes classes for reading and writing a wide variety of image formats, as well as functions for manipulating images. Most of the image manipulations that you can perform with a program such as the Gimp or Photoshop can be achieved using the Image module. The Image module is standardized to the point that other Pike modules that work with graphical data (such as GTK) often accept Image objects as input.

Creating Image objects

The first step in using the Image module is to create an `Image.Image` object, which is the object that represents your image. You can do this one of two ways: either load and decode an existing image, or create an empty image object. The simplest way to create an empty `Image` object is to pass the desired image size as arguments to the constructor:

```
Image.Image my_image = Image.Image(200, 300);
```

This statement will create an empty image object that is 200 pixels high by 300 pixels wide. You can also specify the color you'd like the image to be filled with by providing the appropriate RGB color codes as part of the constructor. For example, to create an image the same size as the previous, but this time filled red, use the following statement:

```
Image.Image my_image = Image.Image(200, 300, 255, 0, 0);
```

You can also create an `Image.Image` from an existing image file by decoding it. Depending on the settings your Pike was compiled with, you may have some or all of the supported image formats. There are two ways to decode a file. You can specify the format of the file, or allow Pike to guess. If you let Pike guess, it will try each format it has support for until it successfully decodes the image. To allow Pike to decode the image as best it can, use the `Image.load()` function. This function takes a string containing the image data to be decoded. It will return an `Image.Image` object if it was able to decode the image. For example:

```
Image.Image my_image =
Image.load(Stdio.read_file("/tmp/test.gif"));
```

Pike: an Introduction

This code snippet will read the file "`/tmp/test.gif`"and attempt to decode it into an `Image.Image` object. If you already know the type of image, you can specify the image format module you want to use to decode it:

```
Image.Image my_image = Image.GIF.decode(

  Stdio.read_file("/tmp/test.gif")

);
```

When using this technique, you need to know the name of the image module that handles the type of image you want to decode. While decoding images in this way is a little bit more tedious, you are ensured that your image will be decoded by the specific image format module you specify.

Manipulating Image.Image objects

Once you have an `Image.Image` object, you can perform all sorts of operations, ranging from filters to drawing operations. We'll cover some of the more commonly used operations. We'll start with manipulation functions and finish up with drawing, text and information functions. It is useful to note that each of these functions returns the updated object, so that you can use it in a chain of operations. We discussed this technique in the cryptography section earlier in this chapter.

`scale()` can be used to modify the size of an image, scaling the contents to fit. The function takes one or two arguments, depending on its intended usage. If one argument is passed, it describes the scale factor to be used. If two arguments are passed, the interpretation depends on their type. If floats are used, they specify the scale factor for both the X dimension and Y dimension. If integers are used, they specify the absolute pixel size for the X and Y dimensions. If either argument is zero, that dimension will be scaled in proportion to the other dimension. For example, to scale our test image proportionally so that its height (Y dimension) is 140 pixels, we would use the following statement:

```
my_image->scale(0, 140);
```

rotate() will rotate an image a given number of integer or float degrees. You can additionally provide a set of RGB colors as the last 3 integer arguments to set the background color not filled by the rotated image. The rotate_expand() variant of rotate() will stretch the border pixels to fill the space not used by the rotated image. For example, to rotate our sample image 15 degrees and fill the background with black, we would use the following statement:

```
my_image->rotate(15, 0, 0, 0);
```

blur() can be used to perform a blur operation on an image. It takes an integer that tells the function how many times to operate on the image. The blur() function is optimized, and is several times faster than the equivalent matrix filter. The following example performs a blur on an image with 2 passes:

```
my_image->blur(2);
```

You can copy and paste pieces of images by using the copy() and paste() functions. copy() selects a rectangle from an image and returns an Image.Image object that contains a copy of the contents of that rectangle. If you don't specify X and Y coordinates for the upper and lower corners of the selection, the whole image will be copied. paste() will paste an Image.Image object into another. If you provide an X and Y coordinate, the image will be pasted with the upper left corner positioned at those coordinates. The following example copies a 10 pixel square section of an image and pastes it to a new image, 5 pixels from the upper left hand corner:

```
Image.Image new_image = Image.load(
```

Pike: an Introduction

```
Stdio.read_file("/tmp/test.gif"));
Image.Image i2 = my_image->copy(0, 0, 10, 10);
new_image->paste(i2, 5, 5);
```

We've only scratched the surface of the Image module's capabilities. Now that you understand the fundamentals of how the module and its functions work, you should have no trouble finding many unique uses for it.

Generating image output

Now that we've figured out how to create images, we can write our image to a file. In addition to decoding images, most of Pike's image format modules can encode images. We can use the encode() method provided by one of these image format modules to convert an Image.Image object to a string containing the encoded image. From there, it's just a matter of writing the file to disk or sending it to a client over the network. The encode() function takes an Image.Image object plus an optional mapping that specifies encoding options for the chosen image format. The encoding options available vary from format to format, the following shows how to encode our sample image as a JPEG file:

```
string image_data = Image.JPEG.encode(my_image,
  (["quality": 90, "comment": "encoding by pike"]));
Stdio.write_file("/tmp/test.jpg", image_data);
```

As you can see, the Image module is both easy to use, and quite powerful. In fact, it might not be much of an exaggeration to say that Gimp's image editing engine could have been written in Pike.

Appendix A: Pike Style Guide

Every programming language tends to develop a set of common techniques and practices that tend to become widely adopted among its user base, and in this regard, Pike is no different. We refer to this collection of techniques and practices as the "Pike style."

Being familiar with the Pike style will enable you to capitalize on the best practices developed over the years by hundreds of Pike developers, and will make it easier to communicate and work with the code of other Pike programmers. Additionally, the more popular ways of performing a task also tend to be more highly optimized, giving you a higher performance program.

We will try to point out a number of the more common practices in the Pike style. Over time, you'll probably pick up on others that are floating about.

Regular expressions versus sscanf()

While Pike has long had built in support for regular expression (regexp) matching and string splitting based on regexps, their use has not been as nearly widespread as that in other languages such as Perl. When practical, Pike programmers tend to use the sscanf() and array_sscanf() functions along with string operators to perform string manipulation. Many of these programmers feel that sscanf() results in more easily understood code. Note that sscanf() does not necessarily peform better than equivalent regular expressions.

Pike: an Introduction

Judicious use of import

Contrary to its widespread use in other languages, notably Java, Pike programmers tend to avoid the use of import. The rationale behind this tendency is that the use of import can result in ambiguous and confusing code. While this is a largely stylistic choice, the effort involved in not using import is more than made up for in clarity of the resulting code. Also, it's worth noting that while many languages have an import statement, they often serve very different purposes. For example, Python's import statement is used to identify the code modules being used, as opposed to Pike's import statement (and Java's too,) where import is used to bring the identifiers in a class into the local scope. In the latter situations, import is a wholly optional operation, though many would argue that Java would be unusable without import, due to Java's typically lengthy package names.

Class and function naming

Another stylistic practice commonly encountered in Pike programming surrounds the naming of modules, classes and their members. Modules and classes are named using CamelCase, that is, the first letter of each natural word is capitalized, and names are written without spaces. For example, a class might be named `Message-Queue` or `StrictRuleHandler`. Class members, such as functions and variables, tend to be named in all lower case letters, with words separated by underscores. Examples of class member names include: `write_file`, `buffer_len` and `program_cache`. Constants are most often written in capital letters, for instance: `STOCK_OK_BUTTON` or `DEFAULT_PORT`.

Classes as files

One peculiarity of Pike is that each file with a `.pike` extension already represents a class with the class name being the filename. To create a class `MessageQueue` you simply create a file named `MessageQueue.pike` and put all its functions inside. This makes object orientation very easy to learn because it is easy to understand files as entities that encapsulate related functions and variables. Because there is no `class` keyword used in this case you may even be making use of object orientation without realizing it.

Appendix B: Installing Pike

If you don't already have a copy of Pike installed on your computer, fear not, because Pike has been tested on many popular operating systems, including most UNIXes, as well as Windows and MacOS X. Pre-built binaries are available for the most common operating systems on the Pike website, native packages are included with various GNU/Linux distributions (Debian, Ubuntu, Gentoo) and FreeBSD. Check your operating system or build and install a Pike customized for your system. For the most part, Pike is fairly easy to build and install. This appendix will lay out the basic procedures required to prepare your own working Pike installation.

Install any prerequisite software packages

The first step in the installation process is to make sure that any necessary software prerequisites are available on the designated build and install system (the target). The following external software libraries are strictly optional, however the presence of certain packages enables many useful features available in Pike. A few of these "optional" packages really ought to be considered mandatory, they're so commonly needed, that without them, you might not be able to run your Pike programs.

You should install the packages you'll need before you begin to compile the Pike package. As long as you install these libraries in a reasonably standard location (such as /usr or /usr/local), the Pike configuration process should be able to find them. If you're installing the prerequisites from a binary package, you should also install any "development" packages that go with the libraries you're installing.

Pike: an Introduction

If you have installed a package, and the Pike configuration process isn't able to find it, you may have to provide a little assistance, through the use of environment variables such as CFLAGS and LDFLAGS, or command line arguments to the configure command.

The following list contains some recommended software that is useful when using Pike, roughly listed in order of importance:

- Nettle cryptographic library (included with official Pike source distributions.)

- GNU gmp (highly recommended and required for bignum and SSL support.)

- Database Libraries (required for database access, choose one that matches the type of databases you'll be using.)

    - mysql

    - postgresql

    - oracle

    - sybase

    - odbc

- Graphics Libraries (required for image manipulation of the formats listed below, most others are handled natively. Again, choose those that you anticipate using.)

- libtiff

- jpeg

- freetype

- zlib

- GDBM

- Java (used for embedded Java support.)

Download and install Pike

1. Get Pike.

Official Pike releases are available by visiting the main Pike website at http://pike.ida.liu.se/:

```
$ wget http://pike.ida.liu.se/pub/pike/latest-stable/Pike-
v7.6.86.tar.gz
```

2. Unpack Pike.

```
$ gzip -d Pike-v7.6.86.tar.gz
$ tar xf Pike-v7.6.86.tar.gz
```

3. Enter Pike source directory.

```
$ cd Pike-v7.6.86
```

Pike: an Introduction

4. Now you are ready to configure and build Pike. Just type `make`, as the Makefile in this directory has all the magic needed to build Pike:

```
$ make
```

You should make a note of the output of the configure process, in order to be sure that it was able to find all of the optional software libraries you installed previously.

Assuming that the configuration process went smoothly, and it found all of the software you wanted it to find, make will automatically proceed to building the software. Depending on the speed of your computer, this can take anywhere from 10 minutes to an hour. If the make process winds down without any major errors, you should be all set to continue. If not, see the next section for tips on specifying arguments to the configuration and build process.

6. Install the binary.

Once the Pike interpreter is built, you can install it. The default location for installing Pike is in `/usr/local/pike/pike-version`. Symbolic links are made from that location to the `/usr/local/bin` directory for the `pike` command. If you're paranoid, you may run

```
$ make test
```

to run a rather large series of validation tests against the interpreter you just built. In most cases, however, that's not necessary unless you run into problems running some Pike applications.

To install Pike, you need to run the following command as root (or as another user who has permission to write to the chosen destination directory:

```
$ make install
```

You should see a series of messages and finally a message indicating that Pike was successfully installed. You can verify this by running the pike interpreter from a command line:

```
$ /usr/local/bin/pike
Pike v7.6 release 86 running Hilfe v3.5 (Incremental Pike
Frontend)
> exit(0);
Terminal closed.
```

This lets you know that you've got yourself a functioning Pike interpreter.

As the alternative to the process outlined above you may install the pre-packaged versions of Pike if they exist for your operating system.

Customizing the configuration process

If the configure process isn't able to find a library you installed, such as Mysql, you can use the following environment variables to assist the process, as shown in the example below using the Bourne shell:

```
$ CFLAGS="-I/usr/local/mysql/include"
```

```
$ LDFLAGS="-L/usr/local/mysql/lib"
```

```
$ export CFLAGS LDFLAGS
```

Pike: an Introduction

If you want to force the use of a particular compiler such as `cc` or to provide additional options to the compiler:

```
$ CC=cc

$ export CC

The following command is required to force configure to look
for things again:

$ rm config.cache

$ make
```

There are also a number of command line arguments that you can provide to the configure process in order to specify file locations, enable features and alter the configuration process. To see the available options, enter the following command:

```
$ make configure_help
```

To provide additional options to the configure process, you can use the CONFIGUREARGS option to `make`. For example, when using the Sun provided `gcc` on Solaris, you must use the `--with-force-ua32` option:

```
$ make CONFIGUREARGS="--with-force-ua32"
```

Appendix C: Solutions to End of Chapter Exercises

First Steps

1a. You have to retain spaces between variable types and variable names, and function names and return types.

1b. Spaces can be added anywhere, as long as identifiers (variable names, etc) and operators are not split.

2. 63

3. The last result is stored in `___[-1]` as well as in the shortcut `_`.

Your Second Pike Program

2. If you enter an incorrect URL, an error with a "backtrace" will be thrown.

3. You can use the `sizeof()` function to get the size of the data:

```
int datalen = sizeof(page_content);
write("bytes retrieved: " + datalen + "\n");
```

Pike: an Introduction

Basics of Pike Programs

1. Sample program:

```
int main()
{
    string a = "abc";
    string b = "123";
    string c = a + b;
    print(c + "\n");
    return 0;
}
```

2. Sample program:

```
int main()
{
    array x = ({"foo", "bar"});
    x[3] = "gazonk";
    return 0;
}
```

3. Sample program:

```
int main()
{
    array x = ({"foo", "bar"});
    // resize the array
    x = x + allocate(1);
    x[3] = "gazonk";
```

```
    return 0;
  }
```

4. Sample program:

```
  int main()
  {
    array x = ({4, 5, 6});
    array z = x;
    write("x[1] is " + x[1] + " and z[1] is "
              + z[1] + ".\n");
    z[1] = 27;
    write("now, x[1] is " + x[1] + " and z[1] is "
              + z[1] + ".\n");
    // now we copy the array.
    array q = copy_value(z);
    q[1] = 4;
    write("finally, x[1] is " + x[1] + ", z[1] is " + z[1] +
              "and q[1] is " + q[1] + ".\n");
    return 0;
  }
```

Object-Oriented Programming

1. A boat class should have a number of values that describe it, such as the length, keel depth, whether it's wind powered, and its maximum speed. There should be methods provided for modifying these values, as well as for basic actions such as

Pike: an Introduction

load and unloading, moving and so forth. A motor vehicle should have settings for the number of wheels, doors, maximum speed and cargo capacity. Similarly, the motor vehicle should have methods for setting and getting these values, as well as for movement, loading, and so forth.

2. Sample (incomplete) implementation for a vehicle (a boat would require appropriate modifications):

```
class Vehicle
{
  static int wheels = 4;
  static int doors = 2;
  static int max_speed = 100; // in km/h
  void set_speed(int kmh)
  {
    max_speed = kmh;
  }
  void set_wheels(int numwheels)
  {
    if(numwheels > 30)
    {
      write("sheesh! wheels don't grow on trees!\n");
      return;
    }
    else wheels = numwheels;
  }
}
```

Appendix C: Solutions to End of Chapter Exercises

3. An amphibious vehicle shares characteristics of both boats and motor vehicles, however some may differ based on the whether it's in boat mode or vehicle mode. We should have functions for setting and retrieving the current mode.

4. We can use multiple inheritance to simplify the construction of our amphibious vehicle class:

```
class AmphibiousVehicle
{
    inherit Vehicle : vehicle;
    inherit Boat : boat;
    string mode = "vehicle"; // we normally operate as a vehicle
    void set_mode(string newmode)
    {
        if(newmode != "vehicle" && newmode != "boat")
        {
            write("sheesh, it's a boat, not a rocketship!\n");
            return;
        }
        mode = newmode;
    }
}
```

Statements

1. Expression statements are used to execute an expression and are the basic building blocks of programs. Control statements are used to alter program flow based on variables and boolean expressions. Compound statements are used to group

Pike: an Introduction

multiple statements together in a logical group. Other types of statements include the empty statement, empty blocks, `return` and `catch` blocks.

2. Sample program:

```
int main()
{
   array fruits = ({"Apples", "Bananas", "Oranges"});
   int ind = 0;
   int siz = sizeof(fruits);
   for(ind = 0; ind < siz; ind ++)
      write(fruits[ind] + " are in bin " + ind + ".\n");
   return 0;
}
```

3. Sample program:

```
int main()
{
   array fruits = ({"Apples", "Bananas", "Oranges"});
   foreach(fruits; int ind; string fruit)
      write(fruit + " are in bin " + ind + ".\n");
   return 0;
}
```

4. Sample program:

```
int main()
{
```

Appendix C: Solutions to End of Chapter Exercises

```
string resp = "";
do
{
  write("pick a fruit, any fruit: ");
  resp = Stdio.stdin.gets();
  switch(resp)
  {
    case "Apples":
      write("red and crunchy. nice for snacking.\n");
      break;
    case "Oranges":
      write("sunny and tangy; oranges make good juice.\n");
      break;
    case "Bananas":
      write("don't slip on the peel!\n");
      break;
    default:
      write("what, don't you like what we have?\n");
      break;
  }
} while(resp!="");
return 0;
}
```

5. A variety of runtime errors will throw exceptions (as opposed to compile type errors). Some examples include:

Pike: an Introduction

```
1/0;

Stdio.File("/tmp/test", "z");

mixed m = ([]); string s = "foo"; s = s + m;
```

Datatypes

1. The basic Pike datatypes are: int, float, string, array, multiset, function, program and object. The mixed datatype signifies any datatype is acceptable.

2. Example function:
```
void write_type(mixed val)
{
  if(objectp(val)) write("have an object\n");
  else if(functionp(val)) write("have a function\n");
  else if(stringp(val)) write("have a string\n");
  else if(intp(val)) write("have an integer\n");
  ...
}
```

3. floor, ceil and round all round numbers; floor to the next lowest whole number; ceil to the next highest whole number, and round to the nearest even number.

Appendix C: Solutions to End of Chapter Exercises

Working with Strings

2. Example program:

```
int main()
{
  string input;
  do
  {
    string output;
    write("give me some text: ");
    input = Stdio.stdin.gets();
    output = replace(input,
                     ({" ", ".", "!", "?"}),
                     ({"_", "", "", ""})
                    );
    write("output: " + output + "\n");
  } while(input && strlen(input));
```

3. Example expressions:

a. `sprintf("%.2f", 1.2);`

b. `sprintf("%05d", 583);`

c. `sprintf("%4c", 64402);`

d. `sprintf("int: %d, string: %s\n", 5, "foo");`

Pike: an Introduction

       e. `sprintf("value: %O\n", (<"a", "b", "c">));`

4. Example expressions:

       a. `sscanf("2.5", "%f", float f);`

       b. `sscanf("92 something", "%d %s", int i, string s);`

       c. `sscanf("abcd", "%4c", int c);`

       d. `sscanf("%s%[?.!] %*s\n", string sentence, string punc);` (note that we retrieve the punctuation as a separate value. We can add them back together later.)

Expressions and Operators

3. Evaluation would be as follows:

       a. `(8+3) - 2`

       b. `(4+( (2 * 7) / 9) ) - 2`

       c. `(9 % 3) + 2`

       (note that the `++` operator in this case performs its operation *after* the value of a is evaluated.)

      d. `((3 + 2) * 4) - 3`

Introduction to Modules

1. Example program:

```
int main()
{
   string s = Stdio.read_file("/etc/hosts");
   foreach(s/"\n"; int i; string l)
     write(i + " " + s + "\n");
   return 0;
}
```

2. Example program:

```
int main()
{
   Protocols.HTTP.Query q;
   q = Protocols.HTTP.get_url("http://www.gotpike.org");
   write("response code: " + q->status + "\n");
   return 0;
}
```

3. Example module file (stored in a file called `mymod.pmod`):

```
int square(int a)
{
```

Pike: an Introduction

```
    return a*a;
}


string kill_doublespaces(string in)
{
   array d;
   d = in/"  ";
   d = d - ({""}); // does this always work? can it be better?
   return d*" ";
}
```

Errors and Error Handling

1. A warning is a notice from the Pike compiler that is not fatal, but may represent a situation that may cause a program to behave in unintended ways. An error will always result in the failure of the program to compile, or throw an exception (in the case of a runtime error).

2. Example application:

```
int(0..1) testit(int a)
{
   if(a>5) return 0; // our "false" answer
   else return 1;
}
int main()
{
```

```
    int a = random(10); // get a random number.
    int res;
    res = testit(a);
    if(res) write("we got a true answer.\n");
    else write("a false response it is.\n");
    return 0;
}
```

3. Example program:

```
void error_thrower()
{
    throw(Error.Generic("We're bailing out!\n"));
}

int main()
{
    write("hello\n");
    call_error_thrower();
    // we never get here, as an error is thrown.
    write("goodbye\n");
    return 0;
}
```

4. Example program:

```
void error_thrower()
{
    throw(Error.Generic("We're bailing out!\n"));
}
```

Pike: an Introduction

```
int main()
{
  write("hello\n");
  if(catch(call_error_thrower()))
    write("Caught an error!\n");
  write("goodbye\n");
  return 0;
}
```

5. Example program:

```
class myError
{
  inherit Error.Generic;
  constant my_custom_error = 1;
}
void error_thrower()
{
  throw(myError("We're bailing out!\n"));
}
int main()
{
  mixed e; // for us to catch the error in.
  write("hello\n");
  e = catch(call_error_thrower());
  if(e && e->my_custom_error)
    write("Caught a customized error!\n");
  else if(e)
```

```
      write("Caught an error!\n");
   write("goodbye\n");
   return 0;
}
```

Appendix D: Glossary

This introduction assumes that you are familiar with some fundamental concepts that are used in all programming environments. Look through the list, and if you don't immediately know what one of the terms means, you should read the explanation.

argument: When we call a function we send values to it. The values that are sent to the function are called "arguments", or "actual arguments" (see **parameter**)

block: A **block** or **compound statement** is a statement that consists of several other statements. In Pike, we use the curly brackets "{" and "}" to group statements into blocks. Some other languages use the words "begin" and "end".

call by value: a variety of function calling where the value of an argument to a function is passed to the function. In Pike strings, integers and floats are passed by value. Expressions are also evaluated and the resulting value is passed to the function.

call by reference: calling a function by passing a reference in an argument to the function. In Pike arrays, mappings, multisets, objects, programs and functions are passed by reference.

class: This is a sort of "module", used in object-oriented programming. Usually a class is a description of a type of thing (such as "cat", "animal" or "Internet connection"), and it has both data and operations: animals have a weight and a color, and the Internet connection can change the connecting speed and close the connection. In Pike, the terms **program** and **class** are used interchangably.

Pike: an Introduction

compilation: The process of translating the source code to a format that the computer can execute. This format can be machine code, which is directly executable by the computer. It can also be an intermediate format, which has to be interpreted by another program.

constant: A constant is in a way the opposite of a **variable**, but also similar. A constant is like a variable, in the sense that it is a sort of box that can be used to store a value, and that it has a name. But once you have defined it, it can not be changed. Constants are often used to give names to certain values in order to make a program easier to understand: `minimum_income_tax` somewhere in a program is easier to understand than just `20000`. Sometimes the term constant is used to include **literals** too.

control structure: The instructions in a program must be executed in the right order, and this order is expressed using control structures. Examples of control structures are selection (such as the `if` statement) and loops (such as the `foreach` loop).

data: The things that your program works with, such as integers (for example **5** and **-3**) and character strings (such as `"hello"` and `"Hi there, John!"`) are data.

data type: Values and variables have **data types**. The value **5** has the data type **integer** (`int`), and **5.14** has the type **real number** (`float`). You can only put values in a variable if the types of the value and the variable are compatible.

exception: An exception is an event interrupts a running program in order to indicate an error has occurred. Exceptions may be caught by a program as a way of detecting an error, and functions may throw exceptions to other parts of a program to indicate the same.

expression: An expression is a piece of a program that gives a value when it is executed by the computer. An example of an expression in Pike is 5 * x + 7, which means "take the value of the variable x and multiply it with **5**, and then add **7**". An expression also has a type, and in this case the type is int.

first class object: an entity which can be used in programs without restriction. In Pike, a first class object may among other things be stored in a variable, compared to other entities, passed as argument to or returned from a function.

function: Most programming languages allow you to divide your program into smaller parts. These can be called "sub-routines", "procedures", "functions" or "methods". A function receives some values as input, and produces some values as output. A simple example is a function called "plus", which receives two integers, called "x" and "y", and returns their sum. In mathematical notation, this would be written something like "plus(x, y) = x + y". In Pike, we write "int plus(int x, int y) { return x + y; }". See also **method**.

function call: When one part of program needs to execute another part of the program, and that other part is a **function**, we say that it "calls" that **function**. in Pike, we would write "plus(3, 5)" to call the **function** plus mentioned above. The values 3 and 5 are then sent to the **function**, it adds them, and the result 8 is sent back from the **function**.

identifier: A sequence of characters that can be used in a program as a name, of a variable or of something else. In Pike an identifier must start with an alphabetical

Pike: an Introduction

letter or an underscore character ("_"). The rest of the characters can be alphabetical letters, underscores, and digits. Some valid identifiers in Pike are `n`, `number_of_9s`, and `DoNotFeedTheMonkey`.

literal: A literal is a value of some kind, written directly in the program. `"Hello"` is a string literal, `-678` is an integer literal, and `({ 7, 8, 9 })` is an array literal. Literals are sometimes also referred to as **constant**s.

local: A variable that is local in a piece of code, such as a function, is only available to the code inside that piece. Other functions can have their own local variables with the same name, but they are all different variables: different boxes to store things in.

method: In object-oriented programming (which is explained below), functions belong to a certain class, and they work mainly with the data belonging to that class. Such a **function**, which belongs to a class, is usually called a "**method**". In Pike, each source file represents a class, so all the functions that you define are actually methods.

object: A class is a description of a type of thing (such as "cat"), and an object is one such thing (such as one particular cat). An object is an **instance** or a **clone** of a class: all cats are instances of the class "cat."

object-oriented programming: In object-oriented programming, we do not only divide the program into subprograms ("functions" or "methods"), but group data and functions into "classes". This makes it easier to write programs, since we can work with one piece (that is, class) at a time.

parameter: A function needs to have some names that it can use to refer to the argument values that are sent to it when it is called. These names are called "parameters" or "formal parameters". In the example with the function plus() above, the parameters are x and y. In most programming languages, and in Pike, the parameters work just like variables which are **local** in the function, and which get the **argument**s as initial values.

program: A program consists of a set of instructions that tells the computer how to do something, plus some data that the program can work with. Programs can be organized in different ways, and are often divided into several smaller parts. (see **class**)

returning from a function: When a function has finished what it has to do, we say that it **returns**. The program will then continue executing immediately after the place of the function call. If the function has produced a value, it **returns that value**.

source code: The source code is the program itself, as written by the programmer. The source code is usually stored in one or more text files.

statement: A statement is a command that is part of a program, and that the computer can interpret and execute.

syntax: The syntax for a programming language is the grammar for the language, i. e. the rules for how the source code is written. The syntax only describes how the language looks, not what it actually does.

Pike: an Introduction

true and **false**: Control structures such as **if** do one thing or another, depending on a condition. If the condition is true, it does one thing, and if it is false, it does another thing. Some languages have special data values, called "true" and "false", that are used for this. In Pike, we use the simpler convention that the value zero (**0**) is interpreted as false, and everything else is interpreted as true.

truth value: True and false are also called **truth values**.

type checking: Pike has type checking, which means that Pike keeps track of the data types of variables and values. If your program tries to put one type of value in a variable which was designed to hold another type of value, Pike may detect this, and tell you about the problem.

value: One piece of data (for example the integer **5**) is sometimes called a **value**, and sometimes a **data item** or **data object**. Note that the word **object** also has a more specialized meaning in connection with object-oriented programming.

variable: A variable is a sort of box that can be used to store a value. The variable usually has a name and also a type. The type determines which values you can put in the variable.

Index

Index